Vicars and Prefects Apostolic

A DISSERTATION

Submitted to the Faculty of Canon Law of the
Catholic University of America
in partial fulfillment of the requirements
for the Degree of

DOCTOR OF CANON LAW

by the

REV. FRANCIS JOSEPH WINSLOW, J. C. L.
of the Catholic Foreign Mission Society
of America, Maryknoll, N. Y.

1924

Nihil Obstat.

†THOMAS J. SHAHAN,

Censor Deputatus.

Washingtonii, D. C., die VIII Maii 1924.

Imprimatur.

†MICHAEL J. CURLEY,

Archiepiscopus Baltimorensis.

Baltimorae, die VIII Maii 1924.

Cum permissu Superiorum.

TABLE OF CONTENTS

		PAGE
INTRODUCTION		1

PART I.

Chapter I.	Historic Origin of Vicars and Prefects Apostolic	3
Chapter II.	Nomination and Accession	9
Chapter III.	Rights and Powers of Vicars and Prefects Apostolic	15
	Missionaries	16
	Religious	18
	Rights and Powers of Vicars and Prefects Who Are Bishops	21
	Privileges of Vicars and Prefects Who Are Bishops	22
	Vicars and Prefects Without the Episcopal Character	25
	Insignia and Privileges of Vicars and Prefects Without the Episcopal Character	28
Chapter IV.	Obligations of Vicars and Prefects Apostolic	31
	1. In General	31
	2. In Particular	32
	"Ad Limina" Visits	32
	Quinquennial Reports	33
	Annual Reports	34
	Residence	35
	Canonical Visitation	37
	Archives	42
	Native Clergy	44
	Council	48
	Annual Convocation	50
	Plenary and Provincial Councils	50
	The Regional Synods of China	51
	Synods	51
	The "Missa pro Populo"	53
	Withdrawal and Expulsion of Missionaries	55
	The Erection of Quasi-parishes	57
Chapter V.	Coadjutors and Successors	63
	1. Former Discipline	63
	2. Present Discipline	65

PART II.

Special Faculties Granted to Vicars and Prefects Apostolic by the Congregation of Propaganda, with a Commentary

PAGE

Preamble 74

General Rules of Interpretation 76

Special Rules of Interpretation 79

De Tempore a quo et ad quod 80

Formula Tertia Minor

A. Circa Sacramenta et Ritus Sacros

1. Benedicendi aquam baptismalem formula breviore 82
2. Concedendi facultatem administrandi sacramentum Confirmationis 83
3. Permittendi Missam etiam in mari, in altari fracto, praesentibus etiam excommunicatis, etc. 84
4. Permittendi celebrationem Missae cum uno luminari vel etiam absque luminaribus 87
5. Permittendi utramque purificationem calicis aqua tantum 88
6. Permittendi thurificationem in Missis cantatis a solo celebrante absque ministris sacris 88
7. Permittendi in ecclesiis sui territorii tres Missas in nocte Nativitatis Domini 88
8. Permittendi functiones maioris Hebdomadae rituali Benedicti XIII, vel una Missa lecta in feria V in Coena Domini et Sabbato Sancto 90
9. Permittendi ter in hebdomada Missam privatam de Requie 91
10. Permittendi Missam votivam de Beata 92
11. Permittendi ut SS. Sacramentum exponi possit cum duobus luminaribus tantum 92
12. Permittendi asservationem SS. Sacramenti sine lumine (ob defectum olei, etc.) 93
13. Permittendi asservationem SS. Sacramenti sine lumine (ob instans periculum) 94

*14. Permittendi religiosis Sororibus lotionem corporalium, etc., et contrectationem vasorum sacrorum 95

15. Permittendi (ob periculum irreverentiae, etc.) administrationem S. Eucharistiae absque lumine et vestibus sacris 96

*16. Concedendi infirmis SS. Communionem non servato ieiunio 98

17. Conferendi Ordines minores omnes simul etiam cum prima tonsura 99
18. Permittendi (in Formula III Maior, "Conferendi") ut omnes sacros Ordines diebus ferialibus conferri possint 100
19. Dispensandi cum diaconis (in ordine ad presbyteratum) super defectu aetatis 18 mensium 101

PAGE

*20. Dispensandi super impedimentis matrimonialibus iuris ecclesiastici, tribus exceptis.. 101

*21. Sanandi in radice matrimonia invalida ob aliquod impedimentum iuris ecclesiastici (tribus exceptis)........................ 108

*22. Sanandi in radice matrimonia mixta attentata coram magistratu civili vel ministro acatholico............................. 109

*23. Dispensandi cum gentilibus conversis, ut quam maluerint ex pluribus uxoribus retinere valeant.......................... 110

*24. Dispensandi super interpellatione in casibus ordinariis........ 112

*25. Dispensandi super interpellatione in casibus extraordinariis.... 113

*26. Permittendi interpellationem ante baptismum partis conversae, vel etiam ab eadem dispensandi.......................... 114

B. Circa Absolutiones, Benedictiones, Indulgentias, etc.

*27. Absolvendi a censuris simpliciter et speciali modo Romano Pontifici reservatis... 115

*28. Dispensandi et commutandi vota privata Sedi Apostolicae reservata 115

*29. Benedicendi cruces, coronas, etc. (cum Indulgentiis Apostolicis) 116

30. Conferendi facultatem consecrandi calices, patenas, altarium lapides 117

*31. Erigendi stationes Viae Crucis et benedicendi crucifixos aut cruces in ordine ad exercitium Viae Crucis................ 118

32. Impertiendi ter in anno Benedictionem Papalem............ 121

33. Concedendi Indulgentiam Plenariam in prima Communione et in administratione S. Confirmationis....................... 121

*34. Concedendi Indulgentiam Plenariam primo conversis ab haeresi 122

35. Impertiendi Indulgentiam Plenariam iis e Clero qui interfuerint Ss. Exercitiis 122

*36. Concedendi Benedictionem Papalem cum Indulgentia Plenaria fidelibus, qui sacris Missionibus vel Exercitiis interfuerint 123

*37. Concedendi Indulgentiam Plenariam in actu Visitationis....... 124

*38. Concedendi ut indulgentiae lucrari valeant confessione menstrua 124

*39. Concedendi ut indulgentiae praedictae applicari possint Defunctis 125

*40. Benedicendi Crucifixos cum indulgentia plenaria toties quoties nuncupata 126

41. Concedendi ut recitatio matutini cum laudibus diei sequentis incipi valeat statim post meridiem diei currentis........... 127

42. Concedendi ut loco divini Officii, rosarium vel aliae preces recitentur 128

43. Permittendi missionariis vestes laicales...................... 129

44. Permittendi missionariis exercitium medicinae et chirurgiae.... 130

PAGE

45. Assignandi pensiones quasi-parochis vel missionariis........... 131
*46. Dispensandi a prohibitione laborum servilium in diebus Dominicis 131

C. Pro Ipso Ordinario.

47. Fruendi indulto personali altaris privilegiati quotidiani........ 132
48. Lucrandi sibi indulgentias quas aliis concedere valet........... 133
49. Utendi ipse etiam in sui favore hisce facultatibus.............. 133
Animadversiones 133

Supplementum pro Formulis Minoribus.

1. Erigendi Confraternitates, ascribendi Confraternitatibus; benedicendi coronas, scapularia Confraternitatum............... 133
2. Subdelegandi facultatem ascribendi Confraternitatibus; et benedicendi coronas, scapularia Confraternitatum............. 134
3. Benedicendi et imponendi omnia (cetera) scapularia a Sede Apostolica probata absque onere inscriptionis............. 135

Formula Tertia Maior.

2. Conficiendi olea sacra cum sacerdotibus, quos potuerit habere; et, si necessitas urgeat, etiam extra diem Coenae Domini........ 135

C. Pro Ipso Ordinario.

47. Asservandi SS. Eucharistiam in sacello domus stabilis ipsius Ordinarii 136
48. et 49 repetunt quod nn. 48, et 49, formulae minoris conceditur 136
50. Utendi throno cum Baldachino et cappa magna in Pontificalibus 137

Supplementum pro Formulis Maioribus.

1 et 2 repetunt quod nn. 1 et 2 formulae minoris conceditur........ 137
3. Subdelegandi suis missionariis facultatem:
a) benedicendi et imponendi omnia scapularia a Sede Apostolica probata absque onere inscriptionis................. 137
b) erigendi stationes Viae Crucis et applicandi eiusdem indulgentias crucibus et crucifixis........................ 137

INTRODUCTION

Christ Our Lord imposed a twofold office upon His apostles, that of converting the world, "Going forth teach ye all nations,"[1] and of caring for those converted, "teaching them to observe all things whatsoever I have commanded you."[2] The Apostles filled with the Holy Spirit, and in obedience to the Lord's command went forth on their mission of preaching the gospel, and as the number of the faithful increased it became necessary to appoint bishops to minister to their spiritual needs. We know from Catholic tradition that bishops were not merely coadjutors of the apostles, but were constituted their successors, divinely infused with the apostolic powers: "The Holy Ghost hath placed you bishops to rule the Church of God."[3]

In the beginning the work of propagating the faith fell to the episcopal office but due to the growth of the Church, bishops later found it necessary to devote themselves to the task of ministering to their flocks, rather than to the work of evangelization, especially when peace had been restored to the Church.

Inasmuch as the plenitude of the apostolate is invested in the Bishop of Rome, the successor of the Prince of the Apostles ought with even greater zeal to feed the lambs and the sheep and to bring within the fold the other sheep which are Christ's.[4] According as new lands were discovered and other peoples found to be shrouded in the darkness of paganism, no one was more solicitous for their conversion than the successor of Peter. He has been accustomed to employ in this immense undertaking the Sacred Congregation of

1. Matt. xxviii: 19.
2. Matt. xxviii: 20.
3. Acts xx: 28.
4. John x: 16.

Propaganda and the Vicars and Prefects Apostolic as auxiliaries.

The gravity and importance of the responsibilities of these latter is impressed upon us when we realize that in pagan and uncivilized surroundings they are confronted with a multiplicity of varied and intricate problems. It follows then that the scope of their knowledge and vision must indeed be broad if they are adequately to discharge the duty of shepherd of souls, entrusted to them by the Holy See. For their proper guidance, besides the decrees of the Sacred Congregation of Propaganda, they now have the *Codex Iuris Canonici.* Many things heretofore vague and uncertain are clearly and succinctly set forth in the New Code of Canon Law, and surely, as the Sacred Congregation has stated, nothing is more conducive to uniformity of discipline and the promotion of harmony than that the rulers of souls be governed by the one law and by common and unbroken traditions.[5]

Wherefore this dissertation is concerned with those matters of Canon Law which are not merely of utility, but of prime importance to Vicars and Prefects Apostolic, for their official conduct and for the proper direction of the clergy and the faithful over whom they are placed.

---

5. S. C. P. F. Sept. 8, 1869, n. 8—*Collectanea S. C. P. F.* n. 1346.

CHAPTER I

Historic Origin of Vicars and Prefects Apostolic

The name of vicar dates back to very early times and in Roman Law we find the title, "*De officio vicarii.*"[1] The *vicarius* was an important official in the reorganized empire of Diocletian.[2] During the reign of Constantine the Great the divisions of prefectures were called dioceses and their rulers were known as "*vicarii praefecti praetorio.*"[3]

The Supreme Pastor of the Church had likewise his vicars or delegates. The presence of an apostolic vicar in Thessalonica prior to the year 347, is shown by an enactment of the Council of Sardica which forbade clerics of other dioceses to reside in that city: "For since the vicar of the Pope dwells there clerics from all Greece flock thither, and often remain longer than is fitting."[4]

In 379, when Illyricum was detached from the Western Empire, Pope St. Damasus (366-384) hastened to safeguard the authority of the Roman Church by appointing Acolio vicar apostolic and Bishop of Thessalonica.[5] Under Pope St. Siricius (384-398) these vicars were attached to other sees. There were vicars apostolic in Gaul as early as the pontificate of St. Zosimus (417) while Pope St. Simplicius in 452 constituted the Bishop of Seville vicar for Spain. Pope Vigilius in 545 named the Bishop of Arles vicar for the territory subject to Childebert I. The same title and duties were conferred by later popes upon the incumbents of other sees, the object of whose appointment was to conserve the

1. Cfr. *Cod. Theodos. Lib. I, tit. VI; Cod. Just. Lib. I, tit. XXXIX.*
2. Larned, History of Ready Reference, XXVIII, p. 18.
3. Gibbon, The Decline and Fall of the Roman Empire, chap. XVII.
4. Eccl. Rev. XL, 295.
5. Ben. XIV, *De Syn. Dioc. Lib. II, cap. X, n. 1.*

integrity of faith and discipline, to remove causes of discord among the clergy and decide all cases save those reserved by custom to the Holy See.[6]

But the vicars and prefects of the New Code are those who rule territories not yet erected into dioceses. As they exist today, the terms are of modern origin nor must we confound them with the vicars apostolic aforementioned. Some indeed would trace the government of vicars and prefects apostolic back only to the foundation of the Congregation of Propaganda (1622). True or not, this much is certain that it was that Congregation which perfected and determined the vicariate form of government as it exists today.[7]

Throughout the many centuries the Church was accustomed to institute episcopal government at once among the various nations which embraced the faith of Christ, nor did it as now is the custom, supply a provisionary government. Formerly one or more bishops would be sent out to preach the gospel to the heathen and gradually organize dioceses and rule them as their shepherds. If the faith was brought by priests bishops were sought and real dioceses erected when the Church was sufficiently established. In fact this custom of immediately erecting dioceses among newly converted peoples survived even to modern times. It was in vogue during the fifteenth and sixteenth centuries as also in the beginning of the seventeenth, in the newly discovered regions of Africa, Asia and especially America.[8]

In the annals of Propaganda, the earliest reference to a vicar apostolic occurs in a letter dated Dec. 17, 1650, when Clement XI appointed Philip Le Vacher successor to the deceased prefect of the missions of Barbary, and constituted him vicar apostolic for the city of Algiers. No mention is made of the episcopal see nor of Le

6. Eccl. Rev. XL, 296.
7. Maroto, *Institutiones Iuris Canonici*, II, n. 756.
8. Maroto, *Institutiones*, II, n. 756.

Vacher's consecration.[9] On December 4 of the following year, the same Pope appointed the Bishop of Belgrade to rule the churches of Hungary, which under the Turks had no residential bishop.[10] But this kind of vicar apostolic may be admitted to belong to the old rather than to the new species.

The present discipline, however, if not inaugurated, was certainly determined by Alexander VII, who in his letter, "*Super Cathedram,*" of Sept. 9, 1659,[11] appointed the Bishop of Heliopolis as Vicar Apostolic of Tongking, and the Bishop of Beirut as Vicar Apostolic of Cochin China. The same letter mentions sending a third bishop to the vicariate of Nanking.

In England the Church was governed by vicars apostolic from 1685 to 1850, when Pope Pius IX re-established the hierarchy.[12] In some countries, e. g. Austria and Prussia (at least before the world war), the military chaplains were divided into pastors, curates and assistants who were subject to an army vicar apostolic.[13]

Besides the vicars apostolic in mission countries there were others appointed by the Holy See to govern dioceses where the hierarchy had been canonically established. They were appointed during a vacancy or when the bishop was prevented from exercising his jurisdiction by some impediment, v. g. infirmity, insanity, exile, or because of excommunication or suspension.[14] Today they are known as administrators apostolic and their rights, duties and privileges are determined from their letters of appointment, or from the canons of the Code.[15]

The term Prefect Apostolic is not of great antiquity. The first mention of it is found in the letter of Clement

9. *Ius Pont. P. F.* p. I, t. l. p. 279.
10. *Ius Pont. P. F.* p. I, t. l. p. 280.
11. *Ius Pont. P. F.* p. I, t. l. p. 313.
12. Ency. Britannica, XXVIII, p. 18.
13. Cath. Ency. III, p. 581.
14. *Wernz, Ius Decret.* II, n. 704; Baart, The Roman Court, p. 325.
15. Cfr. can. 312-318.

XII, "*Nuper pro parte,*" August 23, 1738.[16] An older title is that of prefect of the mission, dating back at least to May 4, 1626.[17] Whether or not these two titles are the same, prefect apostolic being merely an abbreviated form of *Praefectus apostolicus missionum,* authorities are not agreed.[18] In the index to the *Iuris Pontificii,* etc., Part II, t. l, under the title, *Praefectus apostolicus,* are included all the decrees and letters referring to the prefects of the mission, while in the index of the *Collectanea,* they are found under the title, *Praefectus Missionum.*

When the Holy See sent a band of missionaries to a certain region it generally appointed one of the missionaries as superior and gave him special faculties. The superior was then called prefect of the mission, or prefect apostolic.[19] More frequently the prefect of the mission was in the character of a religious superior, and, although appointed by the Sacred Congregation of Propaganda, was yet subject to the Superior or the Procurator of his Order.[20] The office of prefect was, however, distinct from that of Provincial nor could the latter assume that office unless he was deputed by the Holy See.[21]

Prefects apostolic were sent not only to unevangelized territories but also into regions under the jurisdiction of a vicar apostolic or a bishop. To these the prefects were obliged to show their letters patent and faculties upon arrival.[22] It appears that they could not absolve from censures in the external forum, nor grant certain matrimonial dispensations.[23] The precise interpretation of their faculties was apparently called into

16. *Ius Pont. P. F.* p. I, t. l. p. 493.
17. *Collectanea, S. C. P. F.* n. 22.
18. Zitelli, *Apparatus Juris Ecclesiastici,* p. 138, and Vermeersch, *Periodica,* VII, p. (37).
19. Baart, The Roman Court, p. 322.
20. *S. C. P. F. Oct. 2, 1724—Collectanea S. C. P. F.* n. 2250.
21. *S. C. P. F. March 3, 1766—Collectanea* n. 463.
22. S. C. P. F. Sept. 1, 1783—*Collectanea* n. 564.
23. Instr. S. C. P. F. Jan. 14, 1726—*Collectanea* n. 305; Instr. S. C. P. F. Aug. 31, 1737—*Collectanea* n. 323.

doubt and the question was asked whether their exercise was restricted to their religious subjects. A negative response was given. When asked whether their faculties might be used in behalf of the subjects of the vicar apostolic, Propaganda answered in the affirmative and according to the tenor of their faculties.[24]

The consent of the bishop, however, was necessary for the use of the faculties for bination and for the administration of the parochial sacraments.[25] Prefects could not consecrate chalices or portable altars except in those places where there was no bishop or when he was two days journey distant.[26] On the other hand the bishop for a very grave and urgent reason might suspend the prefect's faculties, in which case he had to notify the Congregation of Propaganda and state the reasons which occasioned such a drastic measure.[27]

In order to protect the authority of the local vicar apostolic or bishop, it was proposed in the Vatican Council to abolish this class of prefects apostolic in the territories of the Latin Rite. But owing to the interruption of the Council, no change was made. However, the same class of prefects within territories subject to Oriental Churches were abolished by a decree of Leo XIII, Sept. 12, 1896.[28] In their stead the Holy Father substituted mission superiors with special dependence upon the apostolic delegate of those countries.[29]

In discussing the office of vicar and prefect apostolic prior to the Code, authors were obliged to draw their conclusions from the few pontifical constitutions and the many responses of the Holy See. There was an air of

24. S. C. Holy Office, April 26, 1809—*Collectanea* n. 698.
25. *S. C. P. F.* April 26, 1647—*Collectanea* n. 116.
26. S. C. Holy Office, Dec. 16, 1874—*Collectanea*, n. 1428; Zitelli, *Apparatus Juris Ecclesiastici*, p. 140.
27. Baart, The Roman Court, p. 320.
28. Cath. Ency. XII, p. 386b.
29. Decree S. C. P. F. Sept. 12, 1896—*Collectanea* n. 1953, nn. 1-8.

indefiniteness about the subject, especially concerning the prefect apostolic who differed in so many respects from the vicar apostolic. Today under the present discipline the distinction is more precise since the Holy See usually appoints a prefect apostolic (invariably without episcopal consecration) for those regions in which the ecclesiastical organization is still in its infancy and the hierarchy has not yet been established. His territory is called a prefecture apostolic.

With an increased number of converts and a fuller development of Catholic life the prefecture may be erected into a vicariate; the intermediate stage between a prefecture and a diocese. The vicariate is governed by a vicar apostolic who as a rule, has received episcopal consecration to a titular see, and frequently the letter of erection enjoins that the vicar be a bishop, but not invariably as appears from the fact that a letter of Dec. 22, 1917,[30] regarding the erection of the vicariate of Alaska, prescribes that the vicar apostolic be a bishop, whereas nothing to that effect is prescribed in the letter of June 13, 1917,[31] erecting the vicariate of Upper Kassai.

Vicars and prefects now have ordinary jurisdiction whereas formerly it was delegated.[32] In their respective territories they enjoy the same rights and faculties as residential bishops in their dioceses, unless the Holy See makes special reservations.[33] The Code makes no distinction between vicars and prefects and therefore the same laws hold for both, except as indicated for the "ad limina" visit, and with such distinctions of course as attend the episcopal character which the vicar, but not the prefect, enjoys.

---

30. *A A S.* IX, 99.
31. *A A S.* IX, 370.
32. Zitelli, *Apparatus Juris Ecclesiastici*, p. 128; Vermeersch, *Periodica*, IX, p. (19). Cfr. can. 198.
33. Canon 294 §1.

CHAPTER II.

Nomination and Accession

Before entering upon the subject matter proper to this chapter it is advisable for the sake of clearness to make a slight digression in order to sketch briefly the internal organization of the Congregation of Propaganda, whose institution dates back to the constitution of Gregory XV, "*Inscrutabili*," June 22, 1622.[1]

The chief authority of Propaganda resides in a cardinalitial congregation or committee composed of all the Cardinals of that Congregation chosen by the Pope and known as the "*Eminentissimi Patres Consilii Christiano nomini Propagando.*" Under the jurisdiction of this committee come the creation and division of vicariates and prefectures, the selection of bishops,[2] etc.

At the head of the Congregation of Propaganda is the Prefect a Cardinal, who supervises the despatch of the business or matters pertaining to the Congregation. The secretary, always a prelate, is the chief assistant to the Cardinal Prefect and he countersigns all letters addressed to persons outside of Rome and to all in the Eternal City with the exception of those intended for Cardinals and ambassadors. The secretary is also at the head of the secretariate which is composed of the major or more important officials. The secretariate holds frequent meetings (*congresso*) at which the Cardinal Prefect is present.[3]

The jurisdiction of the Congregation of Propaganda extends over all Societies of clerics and all seminaries founded exclusively for foreign mission work, particu-

---

1. C. I. C. Fontes, n. 200, p. 381.
2. Cfr. art. "Propaganda," Cath. Ency. XII, p. 458.
3. Cath. Ency. XII, p. 458.

larly as to their rules and administration and the granting of concessions regarding the ordination of their alumni.[4]

According to the constitution "*Sapienti Consilio*" which is the basis of can. 252 of the Code, the Congregation of Propaganda may not transact business which has reference to matters of faith, marriage or to the discipline of the sacred rites. Whenever such subjects are proposed by those who come under the jurisdiction of Propaganda they must be handed over to the competent Congregation.[5] Matters concerning doctrine must be directed to the Holy Office, those which have reference to matrimony are to be referred to the Congregation of the Sacraments or to the Holy Office if it regards the Pauline privilege or dispensations from the impediments of mixed religion or disparity of worship,[6] etc. Religious engaged in missionary work are in one respect subject to Propaganda, in another to the Congregation for the Affairs of Religious. Everything relating to religious, whether considered individually or collectively, in so far as they are missionaries, is to be regulated by the Congregation of Propaganda. Whatever has reference to them as religious, to their state, discipline, studies, etc., is subject to the Congregation for the Affairs of Religious.[7]

As can. 293 §1 states, vicars and prefects apostolic are nominated only by the Holy See. The former are selected or chosen by the general congregation or committee of Cardinals of Propaganda, while the latter is chosen in the *congresso* already alluded to above.[8] This will explain §2 of can. 293, which says that vicars apostolic take possession of their territory when they or their proxy present the Apostolic letters from the

4. Canon 252 §3.
5. Pius X, const. "*Sapienti consilio*," June 29, 1908. §1, n. 6 ad 4.
6. Cfr. canons 247 §1, 3 & 249 §2, 3.
7. Cfr. can. 252 §5.
8. Blat, *De Personis*, II, p. 309.

Congregation of Propaganda to the one ruling the Mission, generally the pro-vicar, except in the case mentioned in can. 309 when it will be the senior priest. The prefect apostolic must show the decree or letters patent to the pro-prefect or the senior priest.

The Apostolic letters which the vicar apostolic receives are in the form of a Brief to which others are joined in the form of a Bull concerning his promotion to a titular bishopric. The letters patent which the prefect receives are quite different from the preceding; they are from the *congresso* of the Sacred Congregation and signed by the Cardinal Prefect.[9]

In the case of the vicar apostolic there is a double decree, one is sent to the Chancery of Briefs,[10] the other to the Apostolic Chancery to expedite the Bull of promotion to the episcopacy, according to the prescriptions of the late Pope Benedict XV.[11] Afterwards both the Brief and the Bull are sent to the Congregation of Propaganda, whence they are forwarded to the bishop-elect.

Following a suggestion of the *Caeremoniale Episcoporum,*[12] a Superior of a Mission as soon as possible after receiving notice of his promotion to the episcopate as vicar apostolic, or to the office of prefect apostolic, should write to the Sacred Congregation of Propaganda and express his fealty and devotion to the Holy See and manifest his appreciation of the great dignity bestowed upon him. If he intends only writing one letter, let him request the Cardinal Prefect of Propaganda to express for him sentiments of gratitude to the Holy Father.[13]

The bishop-elect should arrange to have his consecration take place within three months after the receipt

9. Blat, l. c.
10. Cfr. can. 263 n. 3.
11. Cfr. can. 260.
12. Lib. I, c. I n. 2.
13. Vermeersch, *Periodica,* XII, p. (99).

of the Apostolic letters.[14]. As a rule these letters are sent out about a month and a half after the nomination, sometimes later. The ceremony of consecration should be held on a Sunday, or on one of the principal feasts of the Apostles,[15] e. g. on the day of birth, not, however, on the secondary feasts, such as the Conversion of St. Paul, the Chair of St. Peter, those of Saints Luke, Mark or Barnabas.[16] If it is foreseen that an indult will be necessary for this matter, prompt recourse should be made to Rome and the indult will be readily granted if the day suggested is a feast day.

Unless he was in charge of the Mission prior to his election to the office of vicar or prefect apostolic, neither the vicar nor the prefect can interfere in the temporal or spiritual government of the Mission until he has taken canonical possession in the manner described above.[17] Those who act contrary to this law become *ipso jure* incapable of holding the office.[18]

Together with the papers of appointment, the Sacred Congregation usually sends the various formulas for the oaths to be taken, which are the oath against Modernism, an oath of fidelity to the Holy See and the profession of faith required by can. 1406.[19] These oaths are to be taken publicly with witnesses and before one delegated by the Holy See.

Regarding all correspondence with Propaganda or the Holy See there are a few details to be observed:

1) All documents should be written in Latin, French or Italian. Now, as appears from the *Normae Peculiares*, chapter 6, n. 5, any of the following languages

---

14. Canon 333, & cfr. can. 2398.
15. Canon 1006 §1.
16. S. R. C. April 4, 1913, A. A. S. V, 186.
17. Canon 334.
18. Canon 2394.
19. Cfr. can. 2403.

is admitted—Latin, Italian, English, French, Spanish, German and Portuguese.[20]

2) The writing should be clear and legible, especially the names of persons and places;

3) As to the form of the letter, besides being written in black ink on white paper, the pages should follow each other in regular order like those of a printed book, not with the lines running down one page and up the next;

4) The full postage should be paid by the sender.[21]

Letters addressed to the Cardinal Prefect of a Congregation should begin: *Eminentissime Domine* or *Princeps.* However, when writing to the Cardinal Prefect of Propaganda in a gratulatory or an intimate manner, it is proper to use: *Eminentissime Domine et Pater.* The letter is concluded with certain customary forms such as: *Cum summa devotione Sacram Vestram Purpuram deosculans me profiteor et obtestor Eminentiae Vestrae Rev., ssimae in Xto addictissimum . . .* The conclusion, *Et Deus . . .* should never be used except in letters to the Holy Father and with the salutation: *Beatissime Pater.*

On extraordinary occasions of joy or grief to the Holy See or to the Congregation of Propaganda, vicars and prefects should not fail to communicate their sympathy.[22]

It will be found expedient to inscribe the names Rome, Italy, in the vernacular as well as in Italian (Roma, Italia) parenthetically, so that the postal officials cannot possibly mistake the destination of the letter.

---

20. *Litt. Encyc. S. C. P. F.* May 18, 1896—Collectanea S. C. P. F. n. 1929.

21. *Ordo servandus in Romana Curia, Normae Peculiares,* Jan. 1, 1909, A. A. S. I, 73.

22. Vermeersch, *Periodica,* XII, p. (106).

During the summer months the Congregations are on vacation from August 20 to October 10. Even during this period there are a number of officials to take care of the more pressing business; less urgent matters, however, are postponed until after the 10th of October.

CHAPTER III

Rights and Powers of Vicars and Prefects Apostolic

As *Ordinarii* and *Ordinarii locorum* of can. 198, vicars and prefects apostolic have all the rights and faculties which the Code gives to Ordinaries. In addition can. 294 §1 gives to them in their respective territories, the same rights and faculties as residential bishops have in their dioceses, except when the Holy See makes special reservations. The Sacred Congregation of Propaganda grants, moreover, to vicars and prefects, extraordinary faculties of which many may be sub-delegated. But it is to be noted here, that vicars and prefects cannot give to a sub-delegate the power of sub-delegating these faculties. Canon 199 which permits the power of jurisdiction delegated by the Holy See to be sub-delegated, distinctly prohibits further sub-delegation unless special permission has been given. Such permission is conferred neither in the Code nor in the formulas of faculties.

By virtue of the principle just enunciated (above in can. 294 §1), vicars and prefects have the right and duty of governing their vicariates and prefectures in spiritual as well as in temporal matters and to this end, have legislative, judicial and coercive power which, however, must be exercised according to the canons of the Code.[1] Their laws begin to bind when promulgated unless they determine otherwise. The manner of promulgation is left to them.[2]

The Sacred Congregation of Propaganda, Feb. 14, 1702,[3] declared that a vicar apostolic could exercise

1. Canon 335 §1.
2. Canon 335 §2.
3. S. C. P. F. Feb. 14, 1702—*Collectanea, S. C. P. F.* n. 253.

jurisdiction only within the confines of the territory entrusted to him by the Holy See in his letter of appointment, and contrariwise, no other bishop or Ordinary, although a Metropolitan, nor any dignitary whatsoever, might presume to exercise jurisdiction in those places ruled by a vicar apostolic.

Canon 201 of the Code now clearly distinguishes between those acts of jurisdiction which may be exercised even outside of one's territory and those whose valid use is restricted to within one's diocese or vicariate, etc. Thus judicial power, ordinary as well as delegated, cannot as a rule be exercised outside of one's own territory, whereas voluntary jurisdiction may be made use of outside one's territory and in behalf of an absent subject. In the faculties given vicars and prefects by Propaganda it is stated that they may be used validly only "*intra fines jurisdictionis Ordinarii.*" This latter expression then is to be interpreted in the light of can. 201, i. e. the question whether certain faculties may be exercised outside of the vicariate or prefecture, or in favor of a subject who is outside the territory, will depend upon whether or not the faculty implies an exercise of judicial or voluntary jurisdiction.

Missionaries

In the constitution, "*Speculatores,*" Sept. 13, 1669,[4] Clement IX really furnished the *raison d'etre* of canons 295-298 of the Code. The Holy Father insisted that: "Those who are sent to China and the neighboring regions and there constituted bishops or vicars apostolic, should train clerics and priests from among the inhabitants of those places. As the number of the faithful increases, ecclesiastical discipline should gradually be introduced because independence and lack of organization among the numerous workers in regions far distant

4. *Collectanea S. C. P. F.* n. 186.

from the Holy See might easily dispose for the outgrowth of quarrels and schisms which would be detrimental to, and even destructive of the Christian religion." Forthwith he prescribed much of the legislation that is contained in can. 295-298, revoking all privileges to the contrary.

Under the present law, apostolic vicars and prefects must require from all missionaries, even regulars, credentials or other letters explaining their purpose, destination, appointment and deputation. Those who refuse to comply, must be refused the exercise of their ministry.[5] This legislation is not new but can be found almost verbatim in that famous constitution, "*Speculatores,*" already referred to. The wisdom of such a law cannot be questioned, for the Congregation of Propaganda in an encyclical letter of April 20, 1873,[6] declared that cases have come to its attention of wandering clerics who have been received into dioceses without any letters or credentials being exacted of them, many of whom afterwards became a source of grave scandal and disedification to the faithful. The letter concluded with a command that vicars and prefects require from these clerical *peregrini* credentials signed by their bishops or letters of recommendation, without which they should not be allowed to exercise their ministry.

Today, all missionaries including exempt regulars, must ask permission of the vicar or prefect before exercising their sacred ministry, but permission should not be refused them unless in particular cases and for grave reasons.[7] Here, as above, the Code is repeating the former injunctions laid down in the constitutions, "*Speculatores*" of Clement IX[8] and in the "*Apostolicum ministerium*" of Benedict XIV, May 30, 1753.[9] In the

---

5. Canon 295 §1.
6. *Litt. Encyc. S. C. P. F.* April 20, 1873—*Collectanea* n. 1400.
7. Canon 295 §2.
8. *Collectanea S. C. P. F.* n. 186 § "*Nos attendentes.*"
9. *Ius Pont. P. F.*, p. I, t. l. p. 529.

absence of the vicar apostolic, the Congregation provided that such permission should be obtained from the pro-vicar.[10]

Religious

Going back to sources which antedate the present legislation there is an abundance of matter dealing with the relations between vicars and prefects apostolic and regulars, which has been epitomized and embodied in the New Code of Canon Law.

In his constitution "*Firmandis*" Nov. 6, 1744,[11] Benedict XIV says: "As Gregory XV in his constitution, "*Inscrutabili*"[12] has already declared; 'regulars are subject to the jurisdiction of the bishop whenever they have the care of souls or administer the sacraments.' " This the Council of Trent had already established.[13] Furthermore, Benedict XIV in the constitution, "*Ad militantis,*" March 30, 1742,[14] ordained that no appeal or injunction should delay or in anywise invalidate the decrees and their consequences when applied by Ordinaries. This law was soon after extended so as to include regular missionaries.[15]

Changing conditions and new difficulties were responsible for the famous "*Romanos Pontifices,*" May 8, 1881, of Leo XIII,[16] which sought to end some disputes between Ordinaries and regulars. The Pontiff declared that all elementary schools in the missions and parishes of regulars are subject to the direction and visitation of the Ordinary. Other schools and colleges are excepted, permission for their erection only, being required. Concerning donations, the constitution distinguishes

---

10. S. C. P. F. Nov. 23, 1688.

11. *Collectanea S. C. P. F.* n. 348.

12. Gregory XV, const. "*Inscrutabili*" Feb. 5, 1622—*C. I. C. Fontes* I n. 199 §4.

13. *Sess. XXV, de reg. cap. 11.*

14. *C. I. C. Fontes,* I, n. 326.

15. Benedict XIV, const. "*Apostolicum ministerium,*" May 30, 1753, *Ius Pont. P. F.* p. I, t. III, p. 529 §12.

16. *Collectanea S. C. P. F.* n. 1552.

between those which are given "*intuitu missionis*" and those given "*intuitu missionarii*" and the regulars engaged in pastoral work must render an account of the former to the vicar or prefect. These provisions have been incorporated in the present legislation of the Code.

Canon 296 §1 states that all religious missionaries, even those belonging to exempt Orders, are subject to the jurisdiction, visitation and correction of the vicar or prefect in those matters which pertain to the government of the mission, the care of souls, the administration of the Sacraments, the direction of schools, the gifts of the faithful made for the missions and the execution of pious legacies in favor of the same.[17]

Although the vicar or prefect apostolic has no right, except in the cases mentioned by the law, to interfere with the religious discipline, as this belongs to the religious Superior alone, yet should a controversy over any of the matters just mentioned, arise from a command of the vicar or prefect and one of the religious Superior, the former shall prevail without prejudice to the right of recourse "*in devolutivo*"[18] to the Holy See and to the special statutes approved by the latter.[19]

Because of the unusual conditions on the foreign missions, the right given to vicars and prefects of obliging religious, even those exempt, to take up parish work, is more extensive work than that given Ordinaries in can. 1334. When there is an insufficient number of secular priests the vicar or prefect may, after consulting their Superiors, oblige even exempt religious to perform pastoral work. Due regard must be had for their constitutions approved by the Holy See.[20] The text of this canon, "*audito erorum superiore,*" must be interpreted in the

---

17. Cfr. Canons 532 §1; 533 §1, n. 4; 533 §2.

18. Recourse "*in devolutivo,*" i. e. the decision or command of the vicar or prefect is to be obeyed until the Holy See is heard from.

19. Canon 296 §2.

20. Canon 297.

light of can. 105 §1. It is sufficient for the validity of the action that the vicar or prefect consult the religious Superior, and although they may act contrary to the wishes of the latter, due regard must be paid to the statutes or constitutions of the religious order.

Should a controversy about matters pertaining to the care of souls arise between individual missionaries, or different religious Orders,[21] or between missionaries and others, the vicar or prefect should settle it as soon as possible. However the right of recourse "*in devolutivo*" to the Holy See remains untouched.[22]

Newly ordained native priests and all the missionaries, upon their arrival in China, must take the oath on Chinese Rites before the Ordinary or one delegated by him. The documents must be signed by those who take the oath and countersigned by the vicar or prefect apostolic, or his delegate and then forwarded to Propaganda unless that Congregation has dispensed from this obligation. When a priest is transferred to another mission, it is not necessary to repeat the oath but simply to testify that it has already been taken.[23]

Before receiving their faculties the priests must make the profession of faith and take the oath against Modernism. The former is required by can. 1406 of the

---

21. That such disorders do occur is evident from the controversy over Chinese Rites which arose between two great Orders in the Church during the 17th century. Cfr. art. Chinese Rites, in the Cath. Ency. III-617c.

22. Canon 298.

23. The controversy over Chinese Rites regarded the toleration of certain Chinese practices. The question was settled by the Bull "*Ex quo singulari*" of Benedict XIV (July 5, 1742), which condemned the use of Chinese pagan ceremonies and associated rites in Christian worship and practice. Cfr. Ben. XIV, const. "*Ex quo singulari*," July 5, 1742—*Collectanea* S. C. P. F. n. 339, also *Collectanea* nn. 350, 781, 907, 970, 1708, 1900, 2289 and art. Chinese Rites, in the Cath. Ency. III-671c. —A similar condition existed in India regarding the Malabar Rites and the missionaries likewise must take the oath. Cfr. Ben. XIV const. "*Omnium sollicitudinem*, Sept. 12, 1744—*Collectanea* n. 347, also *Coll. nn.* 594, 993, and art. in the Cath. Ency. IX-558b.

Code, the latter by the *Motu-proprio, "Sacrorum antistitum"*[24] of Pius X, which, according to a recent decree of the Holy Office is still in force.[25]

Rights and Powers of Vicars and Prefects who are Bishops

As a rule prefects apostolic are without the episcopal character, while vicars apostolic, on the contrary, are invariably bishops, in which case they are equal to diocesan bishops in matters of ordination.[26] Vicars and (if there are any), prefects with episcopal consecration differ from those who are not bishops, chiefly in the power of orders. One who is a bishop can confer major orders and he is the ordinary minister of Confirmation while those without the episcopal character can confer tonsure and the minor orders only and they are the extraordinary ministers of Confirmation.

Because vicariates are not dioceses, and vicars, even those with episcopal character, are not diocesan bishops, it follows that they have no cathedral and therefore no competency in what pertains to cathedral chapters, nor can they name honorary canons or confer the insignia of capitulars upon their missionaries.[27]

In using pontificals, they cannot act as diocesans, that is to say they cannot erect a throne in any church,[28] nor use the seventh candle.[29] They may not wear the *cappa magna,*[30] have their name mentioned in the canon of the Mass nor in the ferial *preces,*[31] nor have the cross carried before them.[32] However, the Holy See generally

---

24. Sept. 1, 1910, *A. A. S.* II, 655.
25. Decree of the Holy Office, March 22, 1918—*A. A. S.* X, 136.
26. Canon 957 §1.
27. S. C. P. F. Nov. 27, 1858—*Coll. Paris* n. 29.
28. S. C. P. F. Aug. 23, 1852—*Coll.* 1081, n. 1; Feb. 16, 1867—*Coll.* n. 1304; July, 1883—*Coll.* n. 1600.
29. *Periodica,* IX, p. (29).
30. S. C. P. F. Feb. 16, 1867—*Collectanea* n. 1304.
31. S. C. P. F. Jan. 13, 1776—*Coll.* n. 512, n. 1; Feb. 16, 1867—*Coll.* 1304 n. 3; July, 1883—*Coll.* n. 1600; *S. R. C.* March 8, 1919, *A. A. S.* XI, 145.
32. S. C. P. F. July, 1883—*Coll.* n. 1600.

allows vicars apostolic some of these distinctions. In the faculties granted to Ordinaries with the episcopal character, No. 50 of *Formula III maior* reads as follows: (*Facultas*) "*Utendi throno cum baldachino et cappa magna in Pontificalibus; necnon permittendi presbyteris in ecclesiis suae jurisdictionis celebrantibus ut sui nominis tamquam antistitis sive in precibus ferialibus sive in Canone missae mentio fiat: quatenus haec a iure concessa non fuerint.*"

Can. 294 §1 gives vicars and prefects apostolic in their respective territories, the same rights and faculties as residential bishops in their dioceses. Thus a vicar apostolic may perform pontifical functions everywhere in his vicariate, even in the exempt churches. Outside his vicariate, he needs at least the reasonably presumed consent of the respective Ordinary, and if there is question of an exempt church, the consent of the religious Superior.[33]

To exercise pontifical functions means to perform those ceremonies which according to the laws of the liturgy require the use of the crosier and mitre,[34] e. g. the conferring of Holy Orders (even the minor), Confirmation, the blessing of abbots, the solemn blessing of nuns, the consecration of chrism, sacred vessels, etc.

Privileges of Vicars and Prefects who are Bishops

Vicars and prefects apostolic who have the episcopal character, enjoy the same prerogatives of honor which the law grants to titular bishops.[35] From the time they receive authentic notification of their appointment certain privileges are granted to titular bishops;[36] neither consecration, nor actual possession or installation are necessary and a priest promoted to the episcopate

33. Canon 337 §1.
34. Canon 337 §2.
35. Canon 308.
36. Canon 349 §1.

as vicar apostolic, may even before his consecration, use the violet scullcap, ring, and the pectoral cross at Mass.[37] Wherefore vicars apostolic may:

1. Choose a confessor for themselves and the members of their household, who, if he has no jurisdiction, receives it by the very fact of being chosen, and has the power to absolve from all the reservations of the Ordinary and from all papal reserved sins and censures with the exception of those reserved "*specialissimo modo*" and those which are incurred by a revelation of a secret of the Holy Office. The "*familiares*" are those who dwell at the episcopal residence as servants, guests, or for reasons of health, education,[38] etc.

2. Preach everywhere, but when outside their own territory, with at least the presumed consent of the respective Ordinary.

3. Celebrate or permit another to celebrate in their presence, one Mass on Holy Thursday and three Masses on Christmas night, provided they are not obliged to celebrate in the (quasi) cathedral. The restriction "*dummodo*" is understood by some authors to affect only personal celebration and in the event that they were to celebrate in their (quasi) cathedral, they might still permit the Masses to be said in their presence.[39]

4. Bless everywhere with the rites prescribed by the Church, beads, rosaries, crucifixes, medals, statues, and scapulars approved by the Holy See and with all the indulgences attached to these objects by the latter. This faculty cannot be given to their priests.[40] Unlike cardinals who may bless and attach all the indulgences to these articles with the simple sign of the cross, the

37. Pruemmer, ***Manuale***, Q. 121.
38. Vermeersch, ***Periodica***, IX, p. (27).
39. Augustine, Commentary, II, p. 376; Vermeersch, ***Periodica***, IX, p. (27).
40. *Sacra Poenit.* July 18, 1919—*A. A. S.* XI, 332.

law expressly stipulates that bishops use the rites prescribed by the Church.[41]

5. Erect the Stations of the Cross in churches and oratories even when the latter are private, and also in other pious places which are used for devotional purposes. On behalf of those who are prevented by infirmity or for other reasons from making the Way of the Cross, they may bless and apply to crucifixes all those indulgences granted for making the Stations. It is required that the crucifix be of durable material, all fragile substances are prohibited. It must not be too small. Pius IX several times refused to bless crucifixes which were only about half the length of one's thumb. The blessing is given with the simple sign of the cross with the intention, of course, of imparting the indulgences. To gain the indulgences, the conditions are that whilst holding the crucifix in their hands, they must say the *Pater* and *Ave* fourteen times, then the *Pater, Ave* and *Gloria* five times, and the same again once each for the intention of the Holy Father. There must also be a brief meditation upon the Passion. If one person hold the crucifix, a number present may gain the indulgences provided the other conditions are fulfilled by all.[42]

6. They have the use of a portable altar not only in their own home but wherever they travel and they may permit another Mass to be celebrated at which they assist.

7. They may say Mass at sea with the due precautions, e. g. the sea should be calm and a deacon or priest present to hold the chalice.[43]

8. They enjoy daily the benefit of a personally privileged altar.

9. They may say Mass in any church or oratory using their own *ordo*.

---

41. Cfr. Can. 239 §1 n. 5.
42. Sleutjes, *Via Crucis*, n. 57-67.
43. Noldin, *De Sacramentis*, p. 234, n. 199-5.

10. They have the privilege of gaining in their own chapel those indulgences to gain which, there is prescribed a visit to some church or shrine of the town or city in which they actually stay. This privilege also extends to the members of their household. Vermeersch thinks this privilege is to be interpreted in the light of can. 929 where the reference is to any church and not to some special one, such as that of the Portiuncula, or of the Carmelites.[44]

11. They may bestow the episcopal blessing upon the people, but in Rome only in churches, pious places and at gatherings of the faithful.

12. They may wear the episcopal insignia according to the prescriptions of the liturgical laws.

Vicar and prefects apostolic who are titular bishops do not incur suspensions and interdicts, *"latae sententiae,"* unless they are explicitly mentioned,[45] nor are they bound by the ecclesiastical prohibition of books provided they take the necessary precautions.[46]

Vicars and Prefects Without the Episcopal Character

Besides giving vicars and prefects in their own territories the same rights and faculties as residential bishops in their diocese, can. 294 also states that even when not invested with the episcopal character, during their tenure of office and within the confines of their own territory, they may:

1. Impart those blessings reserved to bishops, the pontifical blessing excepted. Among the blessings reserved to bishops are: the blessing of abbots; the blessing of churches; the blessing and laying of corner-stones; the blessing and reconciliation of cemeteries; the

44. *Periodica,* IX, p. (28).
45. Canon 2227 §2.
46. Canon 1401.

more solemn blessing of a new crucifix; the blessing of church bells; the blessing of ostensoria, sacerdotal vestments, altar cloths, corporals, etc.[47]

2. Consecrate chalices, patens and portable altars with oil blessed by a bishop.

3. Grant indulgences of fifty days.

4. Administer the Sacrament of Confirmation, but only under the conditions mentioned above, i. e. within the confines of their own territory and during their term of office, otherwise the administration is null and void.

5. Give the papal blessing in the formula prescribed by the *Pontificale Romanum* and with a plenary indulgence, but only in their own territory and on one of the more solemn feasts of the year. According to Augustine:[48] "A solemn feast is one of obligation which is certainly the intention of the grantor because the blessing is given for the benefit of the faithful gathered in church on such holy days, as the constitution of Clement XIII says." Vermeersch, on the other hand, says that the day may be solemn "*per se*" from the calendar of the Church, e. g. Christmas, Easter, etc., or because of the special pomp attending its celebration and as an example of such, he gives Thanksgiving Day in the United States.[49] The constitution "*Inexhaustum,*"[50] to which Augustine refers, and which is mentioned in a footnote on can. 914 fails to afford a substantial basis for Vermeersch's opinion.

6. Vicars and prefects without the episcsopal character, may confer tonsure and the minor orders upon their own secular subjects, and upon others, secular as well as religious, including regulars, who, according to the provisions of can. 956 §2 have dimissorials from their religious Superiors or from their Ordinaries. The

47. Canon 294 §22 & cfr. *Rituale Romanum, tit. VIII.*
48. Commentary, IV, p. 361.
49. *Periodica,* IX, p. (26).
50. Clement XIII, const. "*Inexhaustum,*" Sept. 3, 1762—*Collectanea,* n. 446.

restrictions imposed by this canon, viz., in their own territory and during their tenure of office are necessary for the validity of the ordination.[51] Vermeersch[52] and Augustine[53] are of the opinion that the dimissorial letters are a requisite for the validity of the ordination of those who are not their subjects, hence the vicar or prefect cannot validly ordain subjects of other Ordinaries before the receipt of the *litterae dimissoriales.* In a footnote referring to this canon, there is a reference to a response of the Congregation of Propaganda in answer to the question, whether vicars apostolic of China could make use of their faculties to ordain the subjects of another Ordinary. Propaganda made reply: *"dumtaxat respectu ordinandorum qui suorum Ordinariorum dimissorias exhibent."*[54] The opinion of the authors just quoted seems therefore to be well founded.

If a vicar or prefect should ordain a subject of another Ordinary without the proper dimissorial letters, he suffers an *ipso facto* suspension from the conferring of Orders for one year, which suspension is reserved to the Holy See.[55] It should be borne in mind that the suspension is only from the conferring of Orders. Hence the suspended vicar or prefect could still exercise all his other powers and faculties.

7. Vicars and prefects may also grant dimissorial letters for the major orders even when they are not bishops.[56]

8. They may designate and declare daily privileged forever, one altar in their quasi-parish churches, provided there be no privileged altar in said churches already.[57] Where no division as yet has been made into

---

51. Canon 957.
52. *Epitome Juris Canonici,* II, p. 134, n. 237.
53. Commentary, IV, p. 426.
54. S. C. P. F. April 5, 1674—*Collectanea* n. 207.
55. Canon 2373 n. 1.
56. Canon 958 §1 n. 4.
57. Canon 916.

quasi-parishes, the church of the principal place where the vicar or prefect is in residence, could be considered as the quasi-parish church.[58]

9. As Ordinaries, vicars and prefects apostolic are not bound by the law regarding forbidden books.[59]

Insignia and Privileges of Vicars and Prefects Without the Episcopal Character

Vicars and prefects apostolic without the episcopal character, while they hold office, and in their own territory only, are entitled to the insignia and privileges of protonotaries apostolic "*de numero participantium.*"[60] These privileges are determined from the *Motu proprio* of Pius X, "*Inter multiplices,*" February 21, 1905.[61]

In sacred functions they may wear the purple habit of a prelate, i. e. *collaro* (rabet), sandals, a cassock with a train but not unfolded even when pontificating, a silk sash with two pendants hanging at the left and the mantelleta over the rochet. They may wear a black birettum with a rose colored pompon and have a special black scullcap with cords of amaranth red silk along the seams with stitchings of the same color. The buttons, buttonholes, cords, stitchings, the two small strips on the back of the cassock destined to support the sash, the trimmings around the edge of the cassock, cuffs and mantelleta, are all of amaranth red silk.

There is another dress proper to prelates which they wear at gatherings and solemn audiences, ecclesiastical and civil, known as the *habito piano*, viz., the black cassock with the buttons, buttonholes, cords, stitchings, etc., of amaranth red silk as described above, a purple sash and pendants, purple cloak, gloves, and low shoes with

58. Vermeersch, *Periodica, IX, p.* (27).
59. Canon 1401.
60. Canon 308.
61. *Analecta Ecclesiastica*, XIII, p. 54. 5 Cfr. Nainfa, Costume of Prelates, p. 145.

buckles, of the same color, with the ring over the gloved finger.

They are free to wear the ring at all times even at Low Mass and at other church ceremonies. They are permitted in the celebration of Mass, the use of the faldstool and the same ceremonies as are to be observed by a bishop celebrating Pontifical Mass outside his jurisdiction, with the restriction, however, that they are forbidden to say *Pax vobis* after *Gloria in excelsis* and *Sit nomen Domini* and *Adiutorium nostrum* before giving the blessing to the people. The blessing they impart is that of a priest, with a single sign of the cross, but they are permitted to sing it.

When going to church where they are to pontificate, they are vested in a purple cassock, rochet and mantelleta and wear the pectoral cross suspended from a cord of amaranth silk, entwined with gold.[62] They may be received at the door by a master of ceremonies and two clerics. Their privilege of pontificating is not restricted to Mass but extends to all the pontifical offices which do not require the episcopal character. The mitres they use are the *auriphrigiata* and the simple mitre of white silk but never the *pretiosa*.[63]

When celebrating Low Mass on some solemn occasion, they may make the preparation and thanksgiving vested in their prelatical habit and kneeling on a prie-dieu which should not be draped but furnished with two purple cushions. They vest at the foot of the altar and may be assisted by a cleric in major orders and two other ministers. They may make use of the canon, bugia, ewer, basin and towel. At daily Mass they do not

62. The pectoral cross should be adorned with one gem only, cfr. const. cit. n. 8.—On account of their wearing the pectoral cross, they should not cross the stole when vesting for Pontifical Mass.—Nainfa, p. 149.

63. There are three kinds of mitres; *mitra pretiosa, mitra auriphrygiata, and mitra simplex.* Cfr. *Caer. Episc.* I, XVII, nn. 2 & 3.

differ from other priests except in the use of the ring and bugia.

On their coat of arms they may have the purple hat with rose-colored or rather amaranth red strings, each ending with six tassels on either side and disposed in three rows.[64]

---

64. Pius X, const. "*Inter multiplices*," Feb. 21, 1905, n. 18. Cfr. Nainfa, Costume of Clerics, p. 137.

CHAPTER IV

Obligations of Vicars and Prefects Apostolic

I. In General

The obligations peculiar to vicars and prefects apostolic are treated in canons 299-306 of the New Code. From even a casual perusal of the questionnaire for the latest quinquennial report,[1] in which questions are asked about rural deans, archives, synods, etc., it is at once apparent that vicars and prefects are expected to develop the discipline and ecclesiastical administration in their vicariates and prefectures, as far as possible after the manner of dioceses.

Since they are numbered among the *Ordinarii locorum* of can. 198, many of the obligations of Ordinaries are likewise applicable to them. Moreover it is their duty, as well as that of residential bishops, to urge the observance of the laws of the Church, to see that no abuses creep into ecclesiastical discipline, especially regarding the administration of the Sacraments and the Sacramentals, or in what pertains to divine worship, the veneration of the saints, preaching, indulgences, and the fulfillment of pious legacies. They are also under an obligation to see that purity of faith and morals is maintained both among the clergy and the laity, and that the faithful, especially the young and uninstructed, are taught Christian doctrine and finally, that the training given our youth in the schools be according to the principles of the Catholic religion.[2]

Vicars and prefects are bound in justice, at least as pastors, to be zealous in the discharge of their office. This obligation is towards the baptized of their region;

1. *A. A. S.* XIV, 287-302, 302-307.
2. Canon 336.

towards the unbaptized who are deemed incapable of ecclesiastical law properly so called, they are bound rather by the virtue of religion or in charity.[3]

II. Particular Obligations
"Ad limina" Visits

In the constitution, "*Romanus Pontifex,*" of Dec. 20, 1585,[4] Sixtus V made a ruling that all Patriarchs, Primates, Metropolitans and Bishops should present themselves at regular intervals before the Roman Pontiff to give counsel and make suggestions conducive to the betterment of ecclesiastical conditions. There was considerable doubt as to whether vicars apostolic, even those with the episcopal character, were obliged to make the *ad limina* visit by virtue of this constitution. In an encyclical letter of June 1, 1877, the Sacred Congregation stated that inasmuch as the constitution of Sixtus V was intended only for those who ruled canonically erected dioceses, it did not apply to vicars apostolic. However, the letter added, they were bound "*ratione officii,*" but on account of the conditions peculiar to the missions it would not always be expedient for them to be absent for a long period and they were permitted to fulfill their obligation through a procurator living in Rome.[5]

Under the present legislation vicars apostolic, not prefects, like residential bishops, are bound to make the "*ad limina*" visit to Rome. Those residing outside of Europe are only obliged to go every ten years, and when unable to do so, are to send a representative or commission a procurator living in the Eternal City.[6]

---

3. Vermeersch, *Periodica,* IX p. (20).
4. *C. I. C. Fontes,* n. 156 §1.
5. *Litt. Encyc. S. C. P. F.* June 1, 1877—*Collectanea S. C. P. F.* n. 1473. Cfr. S. C. P. F. July 28, 1626—*Coll.* n. 24; *Litt. S. C. P. F.* March 23, 1844—*Coll.* n. 989; *Litt. S. C. P. F.* Dec. 24, 1849—*Coll.* n. 1039.
6. Canons 299 & 341.

The "*visitatio liminum*" includes a visit to the tombs of Saints Peter and Paul, an audience with the Holy Father and a written report which the vicar apostolic should present to the Congregation of Propaganda.[7]

Quinquennial Reports

Repeating the pre-Code legislation, canon 300 requires vicars and prefects to send the Holy See every five years, a complete and accurate report of their pastoral office, setting forth everything that has reference to the state of their vicariate or prefecture. This report must be in writing and signed by the vicar or prefect and by at least one of the consultors, of whom mention will be made later.[8]

To facilitate matters, Propaganda, on April 24, 1861, and again on June 1, 1877, sent out a kind of questionnaire which was to be filled out or answered by the vicars and prefects apostolic and returned to the Sacred Congregation.[9] However, in a letter of April 16, 1922,[10] addressed to bishops, vicars and prefects apostolic and mission superiors, the Congregation of Propaganda states that it has been deemed expedient since the promulgation of the Code, to prepare another questionnaire whose prescriptions will be more in conformity with the new legislation. The first report after the receipt of the letter and questionnaire is to be prepared in detail. Thereafter in subsequent reports, such historical details and general information regarding the mission as remain unchanged, may be omitted. The letter prescribes that the report be made in Latin and also that the date be given in full with the year, month

7. Cfr. formula given in the *A. A. S.* XIV, 287-302.

8. Canon 300 §1, also S. C. P. F. Sept. 27, 1843—*Coll.* n. 975; *Litt. S. C. P. F.* March 28, 1844—*Coll.* n. 989; Litt. S. C. P. F. Dec. 24, 1849—*Coll.* n. 1039; *Litt. Encyc. S. C. P. F.* April 24, 1861—*Coll.* n. 1215.

9. *Litt. Encyc. S. C. P. F.* April 24, 1861—*Coll.* 1215; *Litt. Encyc. S. C. P. F.* June 1, 1877—*Coll.* n. 1215.

10. *A. A. S.* XIV, 287.

and day. There are seventeen chapters with ninety points giving a survey of the spiritual and material state of the vicariate or prefecture, embracing the clergy, religious, pious institutions and the faithful at large. From reading the chapter headings it is evident that if exact and truthful replies are given to each question, the Holy See will acquire an intimate knowledge of the condition of every mission in the world. These reports are preserved in the Propaganda archives and are used for reference whenever necessity demands it.

According to can. 340 §2, the year for the reports of the vicars and prefects apostolic of Africa, Asia, Australia and the adjacent islands is to be reckoned from the first of January, 1915, to the last day of December, 1915, so that a report was due in 1920, the next will be forthcoming in 1925, etc. Paragraph 3 of the same canon states that if the vicar or prefect has been in office only two years or less when his report falls due, he is allowed to omit it.

Annual Reports

As early as May 4, 1626, the prefects of the mission were required to obtain from their missionaries a yearly report of what had been accomplished, v. g. the number of conversions, baptisms, etc.[11] Later the same obligation was imposed upon vicars and prefects apostolic.[12] In an encyclical letter of Oct. 31, 1838, Propaganda found it necessary to call attention to a prevailing laxity in this regard and although inclined at first to enforce this obligation with censures and punishments, preferred to pursue a milder course in the hope that the letter would serve as a reminder and produce the desired effect.[13] Reference was made to earlier letters of June 17, 1747,[14]

---

11. S. C. P. F. May 4, 1626, *Collectanea*, n. 22.

12. S. C. P. F. Sept. 20, 1741—*Coll.* 331; S. C. P. F. March 13, 1743—*Coll.* n. 342; *Litt. Ency. S. C. P. F.* March 17, 1747—*Coll.* nn. 362, 363.

13. *Litt. Encyc. S. C. P. F.* Oct. 31, 1838, *Collectanea* n. 877.

14. *Coll.* nn. 362, 363.

and April 2, 1759,[15] which were given the force of law. From time to time Propaganda was obliged to remind vicars and prefects of their duty to submit to the Sacred Congregation an annual report[16] such as required by can. 300 §2 of the Code, which states that at the close of each year the vicar or prefect must forward to Propaganda a report of the number of converts, baptisms, Sacraments administered as well as any noteworthy events.

Residence

The Council of Trent had much to say about the obligation upon bishops of residing in their dioceses. In *Sess. XXIII c.* 1 *de ref.*, for example, we read that "by divine precept it is enjoined on all to whom the care of souls is entrusted to know their own sheep, to offer sacrifice for them, to feed them by preaching the divine word, by the administration of the sacraments, and by the example of all good works; likewise to have a fatherly care of the poor and other distressed persons and to apply themselves to their pastoral duties. All these offices cannot be fulfilled by those who neither watch over, or live with their flock, but abandon it after the manner of hirelings." It also prescribed that were a bishop to leave his diocese for a continuous period of six months without proper authorization from the Holy See, he would "*ipso iure*" forfeit one-quarter of the fruits or income of one year. A continued absence of another six months would cost him the forfeiture of another quarter and should he persist in his contumacy, the Pope might appoint a more worthy pastor to the See.[17]

---

15. Cfr. *Coll.* n. 877.

16. S. C. P. F. Sept. 27, 1843—*Coll.* n. 975; *Litt. S. C. P. F.* March 23, 1844—*Coll.* n. 989; *Litt. S. C. P. F.* Dec. 24, 1849—*Coll.* n. 1039.

17. *Sess. VI. de ref. cap. 1;* cfr. *Sess. XXIII, de ref. cap. 1; Sess. XXIV de ref. cap. 12.*

On July 26, 1662, Pope Alexander VII issued a decree regarding the obligation of residence upon bishops who were regulars.[18] Later this decree was confirmed and extended to vicars apostolic by the Sacred Congregation of Propaganda in a decree of June 17, 1715.[19]

Owing to abuses which crept in, Propaganda deemed it necessary to remind vicars apostolic of their duty in this regard and laid special emphasis upon the teaching of the Council of Trent. It reminded vicars and the heads of missions that whereas shepherds, by virtue of their pastoral duties, are obliged to dwell in the midst of their flocks, much more should it be true of those who have the care of souls in mission countries where there are so many dangers and hardships for the faithful and consequently there is ever a need for the aid and supervision of the spiritual shepherds.[20]

The present legislation obliges vicars and prefects apostolic to reside in the territory assigned to them and only for a grave and urgent reason or with permission of the Holy See, may they absent themselves for any considerable length of time.[21]

In the edition of Wernz published since the Code, it is stated that with vicars and prefects apostolic, the obligation of residence is more strict than with residential bishops, inasmuch as the latter are allowed by law to absent themselves for two or three months each year, while the former, as we have seen, cannot be absent from their territory for a notable period without grave and urgent reasons or without permission from the Holy See.[22]

Arguing from can. 338 §2 regarding diocesan bishops, Vermeersch considers that a "*tempus notabile*"

---

18. Pope Alexander VII, decree, July 26, 1622—*Coll.* n. 146.
19. Decree S. C. P. F. June 17, 1715—*Coll.* n. 285.
20. *Litt. Encyc. S. C. P. F.* April 24, 1861—*Coll.* n. 1215, § "*Quod si.*"
21. Canon 301 §1.
22. Wernz—Vidal, *De Personis*, p. 582.

for vicars and prefects would be two or three months a year whether continuous or intermittent.[23] Augustine, however, thinks that the Code by its silence, seems to indicate that a wider margin must be allowed in missionary countries by reason of the great distances to be covered and the poor travelling facilities.[24]

What grave and urgent reasons are sufficient to justify the absence of a vicar or prefect from his territory for a notable time? Those given by the Council of Trent are:[25] 1) urgent necessity, v. g. when one is obliged by ill health to seek an immediate change;[26] 2) obedience to superiors, e. g. for the *ad limina* visit or to attend a council;[27] 3) charity, e. g. the promotion of peace between factions or nations; 4) the utility of the Church or State, e. g. for the promotion of peace or to give counsel.

Canonical Visitation

Whenever necessary, vicars and prefects are to visit their districts to examine into those matters which appertain to faith and morals, the administration of the Sacraments, preaching, the observance of feasts, divine worship, the education of youth, and ecclesiastical discipline. If they are unable to make the visitation in person, they may send another in their stead.[28]

The words of the Code are substantially those of the constitution, "*Speculatores,*" of Clement IX, on the subject of canonical visitation.[29] Formerly, too, they were permitted to select a suitable cleric when prevented from going personally.[30]

---

23. *Periodica* IX, p. (30).
24. Commentary II, p. 318.
25. *Sess. XXIII, de ref. c. 1,* cfr. also Benedict XIV, Const. "*Ad universae,*" Sept. 3, 1746—*Coll.* n. 358.
26. Cfr. "*Ad universae,*" *Coll.* n. 358, § "*Qui vero licentiam.*"
27. Cfr. "*Ad universae,*" *Coll.* 358, § "*Sane praedictum;*" also Can. 338 §2.
28. Canon 301 §2.
29. Sept. 13, 1669—*Coll.* n. 186.
30. S. C. P. F. Jan. 14, 1798—*Coll.* n. 2259.

The Code sets no time for these visits, hence it is left to the discretion of the vicar or prefect, nor do the canons go into great detail concerning the persons, places and things subject to their visitation. But can. 294 §1 states that vicars and prefects enjoy the same rights and faculties in their respective territories as residential bishops in their dioceses while they also have the rights and faculties of Ordinaries. By the application of these principles very definite conclusions can be reached regarding the canonical visitation when made by a vicar or prefect apostolic. By virtue of the principle enunciated in can. 294 §1 the vicar or prefect, if they deem it advisable, may avail themselves of can. 343 §2 and take two members of the clergy as companions.

Persons amenable to the visitation are the priests of the vicariate or prefecture of whom the visitor shall inquire concerning their conduct, the frequency of their confessions, and their fidelity in the discharge of the obligations attached to mass stipends.[31] If the Ordinary judges it expedient, the faithful also may be examined about matters pertaining to faith and morals, the administration of the Sacraments and the care of church property.

Exemption from the canonical visitation now falls under the general head of exemption and the Ordinary is allowed to visit exempt religious only in the cases expressly stated in the law.[32] All non-exempt religious of both sexes are amenable to the canonical visit.[33]

All missionaries belonging to exempt religious orders are subject to the jurisdiction, visitation and correction of the vicar or prefect in those matters which pertain to the government of the mission, the care of souls, the administration of the Sacraments, the direction of schools, the gifts of the faithful made in behalf of

---

31. Letter of S. C. P. F. *A. A. S.* XIV, 290, Q. 14.
32. Cfr. can. 344 § 1 & 2.
33. Canon 631 §1.

the mission and the execution of pious legacies in favor of the same.[34]

Beyond the cases mentioned in the law, the vicar or prefect has no business interfering in matters of religious discipline which belong to the religious Superior alone. Should a controversy over any of the matters mentioned above, arise from a command of the vicar or prefect, and one of the religious Superior, the former shall prevail without prejudice to the right of recourse "*in devolutivo*"[35] to the Holy See and to the special statutes approved by the latter.[36]

Places to be visited are all churches, public and semi-public oratories, not in possession of exempt religious. Oratories belonging to the latter, but served by a secular priest, are subject to the visitation.[37] When visiting the churches of exempt religious acting as quasi-pastors, vicars and prefects have the right to examine the altar in which the Blessed Sacrament is reserved, the baptismal font and holy oils, the confessionals, sacristy, belfry and cemetery.[38] Cemeteries common to the faithful and to exempt religious are subject to the visitation, not, however, those exclusively for exempt religious.[39]

Ordinaries, hence vicars and prefects, may visit the meeting places or chapels of confraternities or sodalities, even though administered by exempt religious,[40] likewise all hospitals, orphanages and schools, with the exception of those schools established for the sole use of professed members.[41] High schools and colleges conducted by

---

34. Canon 296 §1.

35. Recourse "*in devolutivo*" i. e. the decision or command of the Vicar or Prefect is to be obeyed until the Holy See is heard from.

36. Canon 296 §2.

37. Council of Trent, *Sess. VII, de ref. cap. 8.*

38. Benedict XIV, Const. "*Firmandis*" Nov. 6, 1744—*Coll.* n. 348. ad. 7; cfr. also can. 512 §2, n. 2.

39. Leo XIII, Const. "*Romanos Pontifices*" May 8, 1881—*Coll.* n. 1552, § "*Officium curationis.*"

40. Council of Trent, *Sess. VII de ref. cap. 7.*

41. Cfr. Canons. 1382 & 1491.

exempt religious are subject to the visitation only in what pertains to their religious and moral training.[42]

If the Ordinary has occasion to publish any regulations relative to the observance of the sacred canons in Divine worship, he may visit even the churches and public oratories of the exempt religious for the purpose of seeing whether they are being observed.[43]

The local Ordinary should visit every five years, either in person or by delegate: all the monasteries of nuns immediately subject to himself or to the Apostolic See; all the houses whether of men or women of diocesan Congregations. He must also visit, within the same period: the monasteries of nuns, who are subject to regulars concerning those matters which pertain to the law of the enclosure; nay more, even in all other matters, if the Regular Superior has not visited them within the past five years. He must visit all the houses of clerical Congregations approved by the Holy See, even those exempt, concerning those matters which pertain to the church, the sacristy, the public oratory, the confessionals, also all the houses of lay Congregations approved by the Holy See, not only in those matters just indicated, but also in those pertaining to the internal discipline in accordance, however, with the terms of can. 618 §2 n. 2. Regarding the temporal administration, the prescriptions of canons 532-535 shall be observed.[44]

The Visitor has the right and the obligation of interrogating the religious whom he deems it well to hear, and of informing himself on those matters that pertain to the visitation. All the religious are under obligation to reply truthfully and it is not lawful for Superiors to divert them in any way from this obligation or otherwise impede the scope of the visitation.[45]

---

42. Leo XIII Const. "*Romanos Pontifices*" May 8, 1881—*Coll.* 1552 and cfr. can. 1382, 497 §3.

43. Canon 1261.

44. Canon 512.

45. Canon 513.

The local Ordinary has the right to inquire into the economic state of every religious house of diocesan right and to investigate concerning the administration of funds and bequests referred to in can. 535 §1 nn. 3 & 4.[46]

As regards lay Institutes, the local Ordinary can and indeed must inquire whether the discipline is maintained in conformity with the constitutions, whether sound doctrine and good morals have suffered in any way, whether there have been breaches of the law of the enclosure, whether the reception of the Sacraments is regular and frequent. If Superiors after being warned of the existence of grave abuses have failed to remedy them, the Ordinary shall take the matter in hand. If, however, anything of greater importance arises which will not suffer delay, the Ordinary shall take immediate action but he must report to the Holy See what he has done in the matter.[47]

Canon 345 lays down the method of procedure when abuses must be corrected. They are the paternal and the judicial; the former consists in secretly admonishing the offender, the latter requires a formal trial. When the Ordinary proceeds paternally no appeal is allowed because no sentence has been given. However, recourse is permitted "*in devolutivo*" i. e. the correction must be accepted and the commands of the Ordinary carried out until a Superior or the Holy See reverses the decision.

The visitation should not be unduly prolonged and no unnecessary expense should be put upon the places visited nor should any donation be accepted by the visitor or his companions. All customs to the contrary are reprobated. Custom shall determine the manner of meeting the living or travelling expenses incurred.[48]

For the sake of order and for the convenience of the quasi-pastors who require notice in order to prepare

---

46. Canon 535 § 3 nn. 1, 2.
47. Canon 618 § 2, n. 2.
48. Canon 346.

for the visitation in the prescribed form, the dates and places to be visited within a certain period should be announced in advance, either at the conferences or by letter.

The places and things to be examined on the occasion of the visitation as well as the method of procedure, are given at length in the *Pontificale Romanum tit. Ordo ad visitandas parochias.* A summary treatment of the subject may be found in the Baltimore Ceremonial pp. 399-405.

Archives

Like diocesan bishops, but with due consideration for persons and places, vicars and prefects apostolic are directed to have archives for the safekeeping of the documents pertaining to the spiritual and temporal affairs of their districts. For their own convenience and certainly out of consideration for their successors, vicars and prefects would do well to conform as closely as possible to the provisions laid down in the Code regarding diocesan archives (can. 375-384).[49] Bishops are required to provide a safe and convenient place for the diocesan archives where the various documents may be properly arranged and kept under lock and key. An index of these documents should be carefully prepared together with a summary of each.[50] Within the first two months of each year, such new papers as have accumulated during the year preceding and any stray papers that have been found, should be added to the files. The Ordinaries are directed to make a thorough search for missing papers and to use every practical means to have them returned.[51]

The archives are to be kept locked and no one is to be allowed access to the place where they are kept

49. Canon 304 §1.
50. Canon 375.
51. Canon 376.

without permission of the bishop or of both the vicar general and the chancellor, to whom the key is entrusted.[52] No one is allowed to take papers out of the archives without the consent of the bishop or the vicar general and all papers should be returned after three days unless the Ordinary grants an extension of time, which, as the Code wisely states, should rarely be granted. Whoever takes any document out of the archives must leave a signed receipt for it with the chancellor.[53]

An irremovable safe or vault is to be provided for documents that should remain secret and these likewise must be indexed and summarised. Those which have reference to criminal and moral cases whose defendants are now deceased, or in whose case ten years have elapsed since their condemnation, should be taken out and burned, only a brief summary or synopsis of each case with the text of the final sentence, being preserved. The secret archives should be so constructed that they can be opened only by using two different keys, one to be kept by the bishop or the administrator, the other by the vicar-general, or, if there is none, by the chancellor. Only the bishop or the Apostolic administrator may ask for the other key to open, without any witnesses, the secret archives.[54]

Immediately upon taking possession of his diocese, the bishop shall appoint a priest who, *sede vacante* or *sede impedita*, shall take charge of the key.[55]

When a diocese has no administrator, *sede vacante* or *sede impedita*, the custodian of the archives shall hand over the key to the temporary ruler of the diocese, but if the vicar-general be in charge of the diocese, the

---

52. Canon 377—To avoid possible confusion the terms have been left as they are in the text but, in making applications to vicars and prefects, substitutions should be made for the terms "bishop," "vicar-general," "chancellor," "administrator," etc. viz., vicar or prefect, vicar delegate, pro-vicar or pro-prefect, etc.

53. Canon 378.

54. Canon 379.

55. Canon 380.

custodian shall retain the key.[56] The reason very likely is, that if the key were surrendered to the vicar-general, both keys would then be in his possession.

The bishop should see that all documents relating to the . . . parish churches, also to confraternities and pious institutions should be made out in duplicate, one copy being kept in the archives of the respective church or institution, the other in the episcopal archives.[57] The decrees for the erection of quasi-parishes are also to be made out in duplicate, one copy for the archives of the vicariate or prefecture, the other for the archives of the newly erected quasi-parish.[58] When the original papers are taken from the archives, the prescriptions of can. 378 must be observed.[59]

According to can. 384, the papers in the episcopal and parochial archives which need not be kept secret, may be inspected by anyone who is interested in them and copies may be made at his expense. The chancellors of the various Curiae, pastors and others who are custodians of archives, in letting out documents or copies thereof from the archives entrusted to their care, shall observe the rules laid down by legitimate ecclesiastical authority and in doubtful cases shall consult their Ordinaries.

Native Clergy

As the Congregation of Propaganda declared, Sacred Scripture and Church History bear testimony to the fact that the Apostles established a native clergy among the nations who received the light of faith.[60] Time and again the Holy See has urged upon the spiritual rulers and missionaries laboring among the heathen, the

56. Canon 381 §1.
57. Canon 383.
58. *A. A. S.* XII, 331.
59. Canon 383 §2.
60. S. C. P. F. Nov. 28, 1630—*Coll. n.* 62.

necessity and duty of forming a native clergy.[61] In an Instruction of Propaganda, Nov. 23, 1845, it was emphatically stated that the natives should be trained and employed not only in inferior positions such as catechists, etc., but as real missionaries, who in time might become pastors of souls and even vicars and prefects apostolic. The contrary practice was condemned as opposed to the will of the Holy See and quite out of harmony with the spirit of one called to the apostolate.[62] It is interesting to note in a recent letter of Pope Pius XI that a portion of the Franciscan vicariate of Eastern Hupé was divided into three prefectures, one of which, the prefecture of Puchi will be administered by Chinese secular priests.[63]

According to the Code, vicars and prefects apostolic are under strict obligation to see that worthy Christians of their districts are properly trained and promoted to the priesthood.[64]

In his letter, "*Maximum illud,*" of Nov. 30, 1919,[65] the late Pope Benedict XV emphasized the imperative need of a native clergy in the mission countries for the reason that the native priest has many advantages over the foreigner, not the least of which is his familiarity with the language, customs and mentality of the people.

He moreover insisted that the training of the native be in every respect as thorough as that given to the priests of western nations. The native clergy is not to be established to serve in a subsidiary capacity to the foreign priests but in the discharge of the divine office

61. Clement IX, Const. "*Speculatores*" Sept. 13, 1669—*Coll.* n. 186; S. C. P. F. Nov. 28, 1630—*Coll. n. 62;* S. C. P. F. Feb. 22, 1663—*Coll.* n. 150, Instr. Nov. 23, 1845—*Coll.* n. 1005; Instr. S. P. F. Sept. 8, 1869—*Coll.* 1346 nn. 3-5, 20; Instr. S. C. P. F. Oct. 18, 1883—*Coll.* 1606, n. V; Instr. S. C. P. F. March 19, 1893—*Coll.* n. 1828 n. IV—VII; *Litt. Encyc. S. C. P. F.* Aug. 28, 1893—*Coll. n. 1848.*

62. *Coll.* S. C. P. F. n. 1005.

63. Apostolic letter, Dec. 12, 1923—*A. A. S.* XV, 35.

64. Canon 305.

65. *A. A. S.* XI, 440.

all are equal. The Church of God belongs to no one nation or people and it is only right therefore that Her sacred ministers should be from every nation. Only when there is a numerous and well instructed native priesthood can the Church truly be said to be really established in any nation. Should it ever happen then that a storm of persecution break out against the Church there need be no fear that the hostile attack will prevail against Her with so solid a foundation and so deeply rooted.[66]

The Holy Father bewails the fact that some rulers of missions have not heeded the wishes of the Holy See in this respect with the result that there are peoples who have had the gospel preached to them for centuries and have reached such a degree of civilization that they have many men distinguished in the various arts and sciences and yet are without native bishops and priests. He then commands the erection of seminaries and other suitable measures for the formation of a native clergy.[67]

In the course of a letter to the Apostolic Delegate of India on the occasion of the Catholic Congress in Madras,[68] the same Pontiff expressed a desire to see the people of India ruled by native pastors, nor is the desire of those Indian Catholics for a native clergy, in any way contrary to the mind of the Church in which "there is neither Gentile nor Jew, circumcision or uncircumcision, Barbarian nor Scythian, bond nor free," nor is there any "respect of persons."

In a recent letter addressed to Superiors of Religious Orders and Congregations whose members are engaged in foreign mission work, the present Pontiff, Pius XI, advanced some very cogent reasons for the necessity of a native clergy.[69] The Pope says that the

66. § "*Jam vero*"
67. § "*Hoc enimvero*"
68. Apostolic letter, Oct. 15, 1921—*A. A. S.* XIV, 7.
69. Letter of May 20, 1923, *A. A. S.* XV, 369.

missionaries are sent out to pagan lands to establish the true Church and the conversion of the infidel is but the first step in that direction. This is to be followed by the formation of christianities with their churches and schools, orphanages, hospitals, etc., together with this, the formation of a native clergy and religious of both sexes. If the latter is neglected, the missionary, whose object is the spread of the Gospel, will be obliged to confine his ministrations almost entirely to the Christians leaving the conversion of the heathens for the most part, in the hands of simple catechists. A native clergy would leave the missionary free to devote himself to the chief phase of his vocation, namely the conversion of the infidel.

If in consequence of a war (and the recent conflict has furnished many examples), or through political upheavals, the civil government in the territories in question should undergo a change and demand the withdrawal or expulsion of all foreigners, or subjects of other nations, the Church would suffer greatly as the Catholics, being deprived of their priests, would be in grave danger of losing the faith. Again the need of a native clergy.

Europe today needs priests, and vocations are scarce. It is a great problem, therefore, to supply the home needs and at the same time spare a few for apostolic labors in other lands. A numerous and well trained native priesthood offers the solution of the present difficulty.

The Holy Father strikes a significant note and one which is regarded by many as a contributing cause to the apparently slow progress of our faith in lands where the Gospel of Christ has been preached for centuries. He calls attention to the fact that the mission is not to be considered as the property of the Institute, i. e. the Order or Congregation, but it is a territory entrusted by the Church of Jesus Christ to zealous apostles that they may introduce, stabilize and imbue with life the wonderful foundation of Our Redeemer.

Repeating the same idea expressed by his predecessor, Pope Benedict XV, the Sovereign Pontiff says that the Church is really established in a region only when it is self-supporting, with its own churches, its own clergy; in a word, when it depends only on itself.

In conclusion, it is interesting to note the impressions on this subject gleaned by the Very Rev. James A. Walsh, M. Ap., Superior of Maryknoll, on his tour of the Far East in 1917. He writes as follows: "Not the least of the favorable impressions I received in the Far East concerned the native priests. I met them in Japan, Korea, China and Indo-China, and the experience always deepened in me an appreciation of their strong faith and humility, giving motive to their upright lives and constancy. There were varying opinions about their qualities of mind, power of initiative, and ability to rule, but only one answer could be given to the question of largely multiplying their numbers. This must be done for the spread and security of Catholic faith in the Orient."[70]

Council

We read in the Book of Proverbs: "There is much safety in counsel,"[71] and in Ecclesiasticus: "Treat with the wise and prudent."[72] It is not surprising that Propaganda should have frequently urged upon vicars and prefects apostolic the necessity of forming a council to be composed of several of the more prudent missionaries, whose duty it would be to look after the proper administration of all ecclesiastical revenues and temporal affairs. In matters of more than ordinary importance their advice should be sought, especially in matters

70. "Observations in the Orient," p. 314.
71. XI: 14.
72. IX: 21.

pertaining to the erection of new churches, colleges, schools and pious houses. Vicars and prefects were further advised never to act contrary to the advice of the majority of the older and wiser members of their council.[73]

In the present legislation it is required that a council be formed, consisting of not less than three of the older and more experienced missionaries, whose opinions on the more important and difficult matters the vicar or prefect shall seek at least by letter.[74]

It might not be amiss to call attention here to the prescription of can. 105 §1: *Cum ius statuit Superiorem ad agendum indigere consensu vel consilio aliquarum personarum: . . . si consilium tantum (exigatur), per verba, ex. gr. de consilio consultorum, vel audito Capitulo, parocho, etc., satis est ad valide agendum ut Superior illas personas audiat; quamvis nulla obligatione teneatur ad eorum votum, etc.* In short, for the validity of the action the vicar or prefect must seek the advice of the members of his council although he is not bound to follow it. As Propaganda very wisely stated, they should never go contrary to the advice of the majority of the older and wiser members, for by counsel, hasty and imprudent acts are averted.[75]

Paragraph 2 of can. 105 states that when the consent or consultation of several persons is required, these persons should be convoked and manifest their mind. This is the case with our diocesan consultors in the United States but the Code allows greater latitude to vicars and prefects apostolic and they need only seek the advice of their council by letter.

---

73. Instr. S. C. P. F. Sept. 8, 1869—*Coll.* n. 1346, n. 27; Instr. S. C. P. F. Oct. 18, 1883—*Coll.* n. 1606, n. V. 7, & XIV. Instr. S. C. P. F. March 19, 1893—*Coll.* n. 1828 n. II.

74. Canon 302.

75. Instr. S. C. P. F. Sept. 8, 1869—*Coll.* n. 1346 n. 27.

Annual Convocation

In an Instruction of Propaganda, Sept. 8, 1869, vicars and prefects were recommended, whenever the opportunity offered, to gather their missionaries together to exchange views and so profit by one another's experience. The Sacred Congregation suggested that neighboring vicars and prefects be represented so that the great variety of customs prevailing in the different missions might gradually be done away with.[76]

The present law states that as far as circumstances permit, the more eminent missionaries, religious as well as secular, are to be convened once a year, in order that the vicar or prefect may learn from their experience and receive their advice relative to matters which could be more efficiently arranged.[77]

Plenary and Provincial Councils

Canon 304 §2 prescribes that the regulations regarding plenary and provincial councils (can. 281-291), must be applied, after making due allowances, to the provinces subject to the Congregation of Propaganda; also the enactments concerning diocesan synods. However, no time is fixed for the celebrations of either the councils or the synods. The canons of both, before promulgation, must be approved by Propaganda.

A recent letter of Pope Pius XI, Jan. 20, 1924,[78] announces that the First Plenary Council of China will be held at Shanghai. The Papal legate will be the present Apostolic Delegate, His Excellency Celsus Costantini. The date for the opening of the council was not given but it is expected that it will be some time in May.

---

76. *Coll. S. C. P. F.* n. 1346, n. 9; cfr. *Litt. S. C. P. F.* July 29, 1889—*Coll.* n. 2276 and *Litt. Encyc. S. C. P. F.* Aug. 28, 1893—*Coll.* n. 1848.

77. Canon 303.

78. Letter "*Quamquam*" Jan. 20, 1924 *A. A. S.* XVI, 92.

The Regional Synods of China

Prior to the New Code China had what was known as regional synods which were analagous to provincial councils. In the decree of June 23, 1879, Pope Leo XIII approved a plan for grouping the vicariates and prefectures into regional divisions, each of which should comprise several vicariates and prefectures. The Holy Father prescribed that within a year from the date of his decree, the senior vicar apostolic (the first to receive episcopal consecration) of each division should convoke a synod. He, moreover, was to determine the time and place and should preside. Attendance was obligatory upon all the vicars and prefects of the district or region, but those who were unable to be present were to send their coadjutor, pro-vicar or pro-prefect. These latter were to take their places after the titular bishops, unless the coadjutor were a bishop, in which event his place at the Synod was to be determined by the time of his consecration. All the resolutions and decrees were to be forwarded to Propaganda for approval, although they went into force immediately. Any of the vicars or prefects was free to propose matters for discussion at the subsequent synod and they were to all agree as to the time and place and the one to preside.[79]

Synods

As the Code makes no mention of synods in prefectures apostolic, it may be inferred that while they may be held, there is no obligation. The canons regarding diocesan synods are to be applied, making all due allowances, to the regions subject to Propaganda, it is well therefore to give a digest of them, *mutatis mutandis*, with emphasis on the more important points.

---

79. *Collectanea S. C. P. F.* n. 1524.

As can. 356 §1 states, the subjects to be treated at the synod should concern the needs and welfare of the clergy and the people. In the word of Benedict XIV on the diocesan synod,[80] the following subjects are among those mentioned: public prayers, allocutions, and sermons; the decrees to be read and the profession of faith to be made;[81] the election of synodal judges and examiners and the appointment of diocesan officials;[82] the cases to be reserved;[83] the offering for mass stipends and abuses concerning them;[84] the rendering of an account or report regarding the seminary.

The synod is to be convoked and presided over by the vicar apostolic, not by the vicar delegate except by special mandate from the former. It is to be held in the quasi-cathedral church, unless for some reason it should be held elsewhere.[85]

Those who are to be called and who are obliged to attend are: the vicar delegate; the vicar's council; the rector of the major seminary at least; the rural deans; the quasi-pastors of the city in which the synod is held; at least one quasi-pastor from each deanery to be elected by all the priests of the district who have the care of souls. The one elected must arrange to provide a substitute during his absence according to the prescriptions of can. 465 §4. Others who must attend the synod are: abbots who are actual superiors; and one of the superiors from each body of clerical religious in the vicariate, to be designated by the provincial superior, unless it happens that the provincial house is in the

80. Benedict XIV. *De Syn Dioc.* Lib. IV, cap. 5 & 7, Lib. V cap. 1, 2, 4, 5, 9,11.
81. Cfr. canons 1406 § 1, n. 1, & 360 §2.
82. Cfr. canons 1574, 385.
83. Cfr. canon 831 §1.
84. Cfr. canon 895.
85. Canon 357.

vicariate and the provincial himself would prefer to be present.[86]

If the vicar desires, he may invite others to the synod, viz., quasi-pastors, religious superiors, even any of the secular priests of the vicariate, provided enough priests are lefts to attend to the care of souls. Those invited have the right to vote in all matters the same as the others, unless the vicar, in the invitation, determines otherwise.[87]

Those who, though obliged to attend, are legitimately impeded, cannot send a proxy, but they must notify the vicar apostolic of their inability to be present, while those who neglect to come can be compelled and punished with just penalties, except in the case of exempt religious who are not pastors.[88]

If the vicar deem it expedient, at some time before the synod, he may appoint one or more committees to prepare the matters for discussion in the synod. Before the sessions open a schema of the subjects to be discussed is to be given out to those present.[89]

In the preliminary sessions all the questions proposed by the vicar or the one presiding in his place, should be subjected to the free discussion of those present.[90]

The vicar apostolic is the sole legislator in the synod, the others have only a consultative vote. He alone signs the synodal decrees, which if promulgated then and there, begin to bind at once, unless otherwise stated.[91]

The "Missa pro Populo"

Under the old legislation, vicars and prefects apostolic were obliged neither in justice nor in charity

86. Canon 358 §1, 2.
87. Canon 358 §2.
88. Canon 359.
89. Canon 360.
90. Canon 361.
91. Canon 362.

to say the Mass *pro populo* on the stated days, but rather, as Propaganda declared, January 16, 1803, it behooved them in charity to do so.[92] In a response of the same Congregation, August 18, 1866, it was urged that the expression "*teneri ex caritate*" be avoided and instead to use "*decere ex caritate.*"[93]

Under the present discipline residential bishops must apply the Holy Mass for the faithful of their dioceses on all Sundays, holy days of obligation and on suppressed feast days.[94]

Vicars and prefects apostolic are obliged to say the Mass *pro populo* at least on the solemnities of Christmas, Epiphany, Easter, the Ascension, Pentecost, Corpus Christi, the Immaculate Conception, the Assumption, Saint Joseph, Saints Peter and Paul and All Saints. Their obligation therefore does not extend to all the Sundays, holy days of obligation, and suppressed feasts to which residential bishops are bound.[95]

Vicars and prefects must observe the rules laid down in can. 339 §2 ff.[96] Thus, if the Office and Mass of a feast are transferred, together with the obligations, upon the faithful of hearing Mass and of abstaining from servile works, the Mass *pro populo* should be said on the day to which the feast is transferred.[97]

The vicar or prefect must, on the days mentioned above, apply Holy Mass himself unless he is legitimately prevented, in which case he may have it applied by another. If this cannot be done, as soon as possible he must apply the Mass himself or have another do so for him.[98] "*Si ab eius celebratione legitime impediatur,*" is understood by Augustine to mean not so much a

---

92. S. C. P. F. Jan. 16, 1803—*Coll.* n. 667.
93. Decree S. C. P. F. Aug. 18, 1866—*Coll.* n. 1296 n. 2.
94. Canon 339.
95. Canon 306.
96. Canon 336.
97. Canon 339 §3.
98. Canon 339 §4.

physical inability to say Mass as the inability to apply the Mass, when for example he may have a very special intention, a funeral or a nuptial Mass or possibly he may have a large stipend for that day and no other.[99]

From the text of can. 339, par. 2 ff. this obligation is purely *personal,* i. e. to be fulfilled by the vicar or prefect himself, and *real,* i. e. when prevented he must have another offer the Mass. The obligation which belongs to the pastoral office is considered by Noldin to be one of justice.[100]

In the case of a vicar or prefect who, by reason of sickness or infirmity, is unable to say the Mass, the question was raised as to whether he is obliged to procure a substitute even by the offer of a stipend. Vermeersch thinks that in the case of vicars and prefects who discharge their office *gratis,* there is no reason why they should be obliged to tender a stipend to have their personal obligation fulfilled by another.[101]

When a vicar or prefect is ruling two or three vicariates or prefectures which have been combined but remain intact and are independent one of the other (*aeque principaliter unitae*), or if the vicar or prefect is acting as administrator for one or more, his obligation is satisfied by the application of one Mass for all the souls under his care.[102]

One who has failed to discharge the obligations laid down above must, as soon as possible, apply as many Masses *pro populo* as he has missed.[103]

The Withdrawal and Expulsion of Missionaries

Priests returning home either on their own initiative or even with the permission of their mission Superiors

---

99. Commentary II, p. 363.
100. *De Sacramentis,* p. 208, n. 181.
101. *Periodica* IX, p. (32).
102. Canon 339 §5.
103. Canon 339 §6.

invariably left many of the faithful without spiritual shepherds. Months, perhaps years must elapse before other priests could be sent out to take their places. The results are perfectly obvious and it was to forestall the evils consequent upon such abuses that the Sacred Congregation repeatedly insisted that priests should not return to their native land or leave their mission for another without first securing the permission of the Sacred Congregation.[104] Mission Superiors likewise had no right to expel priests, transfer them to other missions or grant them a perpetual leave of absence.[105]

The same was true of the religious who, when sent out to missionary countries by their Superiors, should not be recalled or transferred without notifying Propaganda.[106]

From time to time through human frailty or due to the perversity of the human nature, troubles of one kind or another arose which required immediate action. A delay of several months, possibly a year, would be the direct cause of grave spiritual harm and therefore the Sacred Congregation very wisely made an exception for such cases. After consulting two of the older missioners the mission Superior was permitted to remove the offender and then notify Propaganda as soon as possible.[107]

Summarizing the earlier injunctions of the Congregation of Propaganda, the Code states that without permission from the Holy See, vicars and prefects apostolic cannot grant the missioners sent out by the former a perpetual leave of absence from their vicariate or prefecture, nor may they permit them to go elsewhere,

---

104. S. C. P. F. March 2, 1665—*Coll.* n. 161; S. C. P. F. March 16, 1668—*Coll.* n. 167; S. C. P. F. Feb. 28, 1716—*Coll.* n. 289; Decree S. C. P. F. Sept. 28, 1812—*Coll.* 699.

105. S. C. P. F. Feb. 28, 1716—*Coll.* n. 289; Instr. S. C. P. F. Sept. 8, 1869—*Coll.* 1346 n 1.

106. S. C. P. F. May 8, 1628—*Coll.* n. 39.

107. S. C. P. F. March 16, 1668—*Coll.* n. 167.

or expel them. When a missioner has given public scandal, after having advised with their consultors, and if the offender is a religious, after notifying his Superior, they may remove him and notify the Holy See as soon as possible.[108]

The Erection of Quasi-Parishes

In those places where the parish churches had no definite boundaries, and consequently the rectors had no parishioners of their own but administered the sacraments indiscriminately to all who desired them, the Council of Trent required the bishops to divide the people into parishes with definite boundaries and with their own parish priests. Furthermore it was prescribed that the same should be done as soon as possible in those places where as yet, there were no parish churches.[109] In his constitution, "*Ad militantis,*" March 30, 1742, Benedict XIV insisted that the prescriptions of the Council of Trent just cited should be observed.[110]

In the present legislation of the Code, it is stated that whenever it can conveniently be done, vicariates and prefectures are to be divided into distinct territorial sections, each of which shall have its own church to which the people of that district shall belong. Each church shall be presided over by a local pastor to whom the care of souls is committed.[111] In vicariates and prefectures these districts are to be known as quasi-parishes and the priests assigned to them, quasi-pastors.[112]

From an Instruction of the Sacred Congregation of Propaganda, it appears that a number of vicars and prefects had proposed *dubia* to the Congregation

---

108. Canon 307.
109. Council of Trent, *Sess. XXIV, de ref. c. 13.*
110. *C. I. C. Fontes* n. 326 § 16.
111. Canon 216 §1, 2.
112. Canons 216 §3; 451 §2 n. 1.

regarding quasi-parishes and their mode of erection. Propaganda therefore judged it opportune to lay down certain rules for their guidance and these will be treated here at some length as they are of considerable practical moment.[113]

The Instruction makes it plain that the Sacred Congregation does not wish to be too inconsiderate in its insistence on the erection of quasi-parishes, especially when it is foreseen that the requirements are lacking. However, even if the proper endowment or income mentioned in can. 1410, cannot be expected, it is not forbidden to erect quasi-parishes if it is prudently foreseen that the necessary revenues will be forthcoming from another source.[114] Moreover, it is neither necessary nor advisable to wait until the whole vicariate or prefecture can be divided into quasi-parishes, but rather that it be done gradually, one or more sections being thus divided while the division of the portion remaining could be put off until a more opportune moment. On this point, however, vicars and prefects will be guided by what is of greatest benefit to the faithful and to the progress of the Church in those regions. The matter should be given thoughtful consideration and the opinion of their council obtained according to can. 302, or of the principal missionaries on the occasion of the annual convocation mentioned in can. 303.[115]

A decree of the Ordinary giving the geographical limits is required for the erection of a quasi-parish. When this would not be practical, it is sufficient to state just what christianities belong to the quasi-parish. The decree should also mention the principal church and the residence of the quasi-pastor. Two copies of the decree are necessary, one for the archives of the vicariate or

113. Instr. S. C. P. F. July 25, 1920, *A. A. S.* XII, 331.
114. Canon 1415 §3.
115. Instr. S. C. P. F. July 25, 1920, *A. A. S.* XXI. 331, n. 2, 3.

prefecture and the other for the archives of the quasi-parish.[116]

Once the quasi-parish is established, the rights and obligations of a quasi-pastor become operative *ipso facto.* The Code states that priests who govern quasi-parishes are equal to pastors in the matter of parochial rights and obligations and in law are known as parish priests.[117] There are a few exceptions to this general rule. For example all quasi-pastors are removable,[118] and secondly they are obliged to apply the Holy Mass for their people only on the days mentioned in can. 306, viz., Christmas, Epiphany, Easter, the Ascension, Pentecost, Corpus Christi, the Immaculate Conception, the Assumption, Saint Joseph, Saints Peter and Paul, and All Saints.[119]

Quasi-parishes are liable to the seminary tax or assessment mentioned in can. 1356.

The functions reserved to the pastor, his rights to the revenues and the obligations incumbent upon him, are treated in can. 462-470.

Quasi-pastors of the secular clergy are appointed by the Ordinary of the vicariate or prefecture, after having consulted the members of his council, after the manner described in can. 302.[120] The text, "*audito Consilio,*" of can. 457, requires for the validity of the act, that the Ordinary seek the advice of his counsellors at least by letter.[121]

When parishes are entrusted to a Religious Order, the respective superior shall present a priest of his community to the Ordinary and the latter shall invest him according to can. 459 §2.[122]

---

116. Instr. *ut supra,* nn. 4, 5.
117. Canon 451 §2.
118. Canon 454 §4.
119. Canon 446 §1.
120. Canon 457.
121. Cfr. canons 105 & 302.
122. Canon 456.

The Ordinary is bound in conscience to give the vacant parish to the priest whom he judges best qualified. The fitness of a candidate should not be judged by his learning only, but the other qualities required for the proper administration of a parish, should also be given consideration. Hence the Ordinary should not neglect to gather information from any source concerning the character of the priest in question, v. g. from the documents in the archives of the vicariate or prefecture, or, if he deems it expedient, he may seek information from outside the vicariate or prefecture. He should, moreover, refer to the junior clergy examination and also subject the candidate to an examination in the presence of the synodal examiners unless, with their consent, the Ordinary wishes to dispense him therefrom, when, for example, the priest is well known for his theological learning.[123]

Where appointments to parishes are made by means of the *concursus*, whether that described in the "*Cum illud*" of Benedict XIV,[124] or a general *concursus*, this method shall be followed until the Holy See decrees otherwise.[125]

The pastor assumes the care of souls from the moment of his taking possession. The manner of taking possession may, according to can. 1444, be regulated by particular law or custom. Before taking possession or in the act of taking possession he must make the profession of faith prescribed by can. 1406, par. 1, no. 7.[126] The oath against Modernism is also required according to the prescriptions of the *Motu proprio*, "*Sacrorum Antistitum*," of Pope Pius X.[127]

A matter of great importance apropos of the present subject of quasi-parishes, is the question of delegation to

---

123. Canon 459 §1-3.
124. *Collectanea S. C. P. F.* n. 340.
125. Canon 459 §4.
126. Canon 461.
127. *A. A. S.* X, 136.

assist at marriages. As regards the form of marriage, the new law states that only those marriages are valid which are contracted before the pastor, or the Ordinary, or a priest delegated by either, and at least two witnesses; due regard being paid to the rules expressed in can. 1095-1103 and to the exceptions contained in canons 1098 and 1099.[128]

The pastor and the Ordinary may validly assist at a marriage only within the limits of their territory and while indeed they may, in a specific case, grant permission to a priest to assist validly within their territory, all general delegations, except in the case of assistant priests (*vicarii cooperatores*), are excluded.[129]

Now as long as the vicariate or prefecture is not divided into quasi-parishes, all the missionaries engaged in the sacred ministry are, as it were, assistants (*vicarii cooperatores*) of the vicar or prefect in the sense that they may be authorized to witness any and all marriages in the vicariate or prefecture. Once the division is made into quasi-parishes, only the quasi-pastor and the Ordinary are qualified to assist validly at the marriages within the limits of the quasi-parish. All general delegations are excluded except in the case of the assistant priest (*vicarius cooperator*) of the quasi-pastor.

If there is only a partial division of the vicariate or prefecture into quasi-parishes, the yet undivided portion is, as it were, a large parish of which the missionaries are the *vicarii cooperatores* of the vicar or prefect and hence they may receive general delegation to witness any and all marriages within the undivided portion of the vicariate or prefecture.

As the Instruction states, upon the erection of a quasi-parish all subsidiary churches, chapels or oratories located within its confines, come under the authority and

---

128. Canon 1094.

129. Cfr. canons 1095 & 1096 §1.

care of the quasi-pastor until such time as they either become parts of new parishes or are exempted from his care in the manner described in can. 464.[130]

The Sacred Congregation considers it advisable, once quasi-parishes have been established, to divide the vicariate or prefecture into districts each comprising several parishes. This has been done in several vicariates already.[131] These districts or deaneries presided over by the dean will greatly facilitate the administration and government of the vicariate or prefecture.[132]

---

130. Instr. S. C. P. F. July 25, 1920, *A. A. S.* XII, 331, n. 8.
131. Cfr. Instr. S. C. P. F. Oct. 18, 1883, n. XII.
132. Instr, S. C. P. F. July 25, 1920, *A. A. S.* XII, 331 n. 9.

CHAPTER V

Coadjutors and Successors

Former Discipline

Since by death, recall or other circumstances, vicars and prefects may lose their office or be impeded in the exercise of their jurisdiction, Benedict XIV, in his constitutions, "*Ex sublimi*"[1] and "*Quam ex sublimi,*"[2] had provided that the vicariate or prefecture should not be left without a ruler, nor the flock without a shepherd. The provisions of these constitutions have been practically adopted by the Code, canons 309-310.

Benedict XIV required vicars apostolic without a coadjutor or successor, to appoint a vicar-general who, after their death, should assume charge of the vicariate with all the rights and faculties of the vicar apostolic with the exception of those which required episcopal consecration, or which could not be exercised without the use of sacred oils. When necessity required it, they were permitted to consecrate chalices, patens and portable altars with oil blessed by a bishop.[3]

Although no express mention is made of prefects apostolic, they were doubtless included among those whom the Pope refers to as vicars apostolic without the episcopal character.[4]

To meet all possible contingencies, the vicars apostolic of India who had neither a coadjutor nor a vicar-general, were allowed by the Congregation of Propaganda, on May 20, 1786, to appoint two pro-vicars, one of whom was to succeed the vicar apostolic. Two were

1. Jan. 26, 1753—*Collectanea S. C. P. F.* n. 387.
2. Aug. 8, 1755—*Coll. S. C. P. F.* n. 396.
3. "*Quam ex sublimi*" Aug. 8, 1755—*Coll. S. C. P. F.* n. 396.
4. "*Quam ex sublimi*" § "*Porro.*"

permitted in order that the vicariate would not be left without a ruler, if one died or became incapacitated.[5]

While the vicar apostolic lived they were to assist him in the discharge of his office, and he could delegate to them his ordinary and extraordinary faculties, except of course any which required the episcopal character. Furthermore, Propaganda allowed the pro-vicars to further sub-delegate the extraordinary faculties to the missionaries.[6]

During his administration of the vicariate, the pro-vicar was not permitted to administer the sacrament of confirmation until he had obtained this faculty from Propaganda.[7] He, too, was obliged to appoint one of the priests as his successor. Should either appointment, by vicar or pro-vicar, have been neglected, the senior of the vicariate, i. e. the priest longest on the missions, or if there were several of equal seniority the one longest in the priesthood was to be considered as delegated by the Holy See to assume the reins.[8] It was later stipulated that the senior priest was to be from that Order or Society to which the mission was entrusted.[9]

It sometimes happened that difficulties arose over the question of seniority and the right of succession, and occasionally, too, there was an antipathy on the part of the pagans against the pro-vicar which made it dangerous for him to assume control. In these circumstances the nearest vicar apostolic was given the necessary powers for the proper administration of the vacant vicariate.[10]

---

5. Decree S. C. P. F. May 20, 1786—*Collectanea* n. 583.
6. S. C. P. F. Dec. 9, 1822—*Collectanea* n. 777 ad 2.
7. Sept. 12, 1821—*Collectanea* n. 766.
8. Decree S. C. P. F. Sept. 19, 1787—*Collectanea* n. 591.
9. *Litt. S. C. P. F.* Sept. 29, 1827—*Collectanea* n. 800.
10. S. C. P. F. July 2, 1827—*Collectanea* n. 797.

PRESENT DISCIPLINE

Immediately upon entering their territory and assuming the reins of government, vicars and prefects are to appoint a suitable cleric as pro-vicar or pro-prefect, unless the Holy See has assigned a coadjutor with the right of succession.[11] The pro-vicar or pro-prefect has no power during the lifetime of the vicar or prefect, except in so far as the latter has committed it to him. But in case they ceased to officiate or if their jurisdiction were impeded according to the norm of can. 429 §1, i. e. by captivity, exile, inability, etc., the pro-vicar or the pro-prefect would assume control and act as administrator until the Holy See provided otherwise.[12]

A pro-vicar or pro-prefect who has succeeded the vicar or prefect proper, shall immediately appoint one of the priests as administrator.[13] Should either appointment, by vicar or pro-vicar, prefect or pro-prefect, have been neglected, then the senior of the vicariate or prefecture, i. e. the priest who is present in the territory and has first shown the papers of his missionary appointment, must be looked upon as delegated by the Holy See to assume the reins.[14]

Those who rule a vicariate or prefecture *ad interim* are obliged to make this fact known to the Apostolic See, i. e. to Propaganda, as soon as possible. In the meantime they have all the faculties, ordinary and delegated, enjoyed by the vicar or prefect himself, except those which were purely personal.[15] Unlike the pro-vicar under the old legislation, he can therefore administer confirmation.[16]

---

11. Canon 309 §1.
12. Canon 309 §2.
13. Canon 309 §3.
14. Canon 309 §4.
15. Canon 310.
16. S. C. P. F. Sept. 12, 1821—*Collectanea* n. 766 and cfr. can. 782 §2, 3.

One who is for a definite time in charge of a vicariate or prefecture must continue his administration with all the faculties granted to him until his successor has taken canonical possession, even though this happen after his own term has expired.[17] The faculties enjoyed by the pro-vicar or pro-prefect are those of the vicar or prefect and have been discussed in other chapters of this work. Vicars and prefects take canonical possession of their territory when the former present their apostolic letters, the latter their decree or letters patent, to the one in charge.[18]

May a vicar or prefect apostolic appoint a vicar general? It seems from the letter that not a few thought so by inference from can. 294 §1, which gives them the rights and faculties of residential bishops, especially, too, in view of the fact that previous to the Code, vicars apostolic had the right of choosing a vicar general, who upon their death became pro-vicar, with all the faculties of the vicar apostolic, and who during their lifetime would share in their office and enjoy the faculties ordinary and delegated together with the power of subdelegation.[19]

But in a letter of Dec. 8, 1919,[20] addressed to vicars apostolic, Propaganda denied that the common law gave them the right of choosing a vicar-general properly so called. This appears to be a logical deduction from can. 198, which enumerates the *Ordinarii locorum* and mentions the vicars-general of residential bishops, abbots and prelates *nullius*, but is silent regarding those of vicars and prefects apostolic.

On November 6, 1919, the Holy Father granted a *sanatio* for all those invalid acts of jurisdiction exer-

---

17. Canon 311.
18. Canon 293 §2.
19. Benedict XIV "*Ex sublimi*," Jan. 26, 1753—*Collectanea* n. 387; "*Quam ex Sublimi*" Aug. 8, 1755—*Collectanea* n. 396; S. C. P. F. Dec. 9, 1822—*Collectanea* n. 777.
20. *A. A. S.* XII, 120.

cised by missionaries who thought themselves to be real vicars-general. The same grant gave Ordinaries of the missions the right of appointing one or more *vicars delegate* according as the diversity of rites or the size of the mission required. The letter referred to reads, in part, as follows:

Reverendissime Domine,

Juxta can. 198 *Codicis I. C. Vicariis et Praefectis Apostolicis jus non competit sibi eligendi Vicarium Generalem sicut fas est Episcopis Residentialibus; . . . SS. D. N. Benedictus divina Prov. PP. XV. . . . haec in bonum Missionum sua benignitate concessit:* I. *Sanavit nullitatem actuum jurisdictionum positorum ab illis missionariis qui forsan ut vere Vicarios Generales se gesserunt.* II. *Elargitus est Ordinariis Missionum potestatem nominandi Vicarium Delegatum si eo indigeant, cui practice concessa sit jurisdictio in spiritualibus et temporalibus, qua ex Codice I. C. uti potest Vicarius Generalis in diocesi.*

Ex hac concessione, omnibus Superioribus Missionum facta, nunc tu poteris Vicarium Delegatum nominare, qui gaudeat omnibus facultatibus Vicario Generali tributis ad normam can. 368 §1, 2.

De numero autem et de officio Vicariorum Delegatorum in unaquaque Missione eadem valeant quae de Vicario Generali in Codice I. C. statuta sunt (*can.* 366, *et seq.*). *Quae dum tibi communico, Deum precor ut te sospitem incolumemque servet.*

Romae die decembris 8, 1919.

What is the nature of the jurisdiction enjoyed by the vicar delegate? From the letter of Benedict XV it appears that he is not simply a *delegatus "ad universitatem negotiorum."* On the contrary, his jurisdiction is connected with the office in the sense that it goes by right with the appointment to the office, as the letter states: *"de officio Vicariorum Delegatorum* . . .

eadem valeant quae de Vicario Generali in Codice I. C. statuta sunt," and therefore like the vicar general, the vicar delegate is an *Ordinarius.*[21]

Wherefore the vicar delegate may sub-delegate to the missionaries those extraordinary faculties granted to vicars and prefects apostolic by the Sacred Congregation of Propaganda. There is nothing to prevent him from being appointed pro-vicar or pro-prefect.

Is there any conflict between the prerogatives of the pro-vicar or pro-prefect and the vicar delegate with respect to succession? The answer is not to be found in the canon of the Code on succession (can. 309 §2), as the power of appointing vicars delegate was given subsequently to the promulgation of the Code which makes no mention of such an office.

When the pro-vicar or the pro-prefect is at the same time, the vicar delegate, no difficulty can arise. But, when the offices are given to two distinct persons, it is necessary to decide which of them has attached to it the right of succession. On this question, Vermeersch says that since, properly speaking, the vicar delegate is not a vicar general, he does not constitute one moral person with the vicar or prefect nor does his jurisdiction cease, nor is it suspended with that of the latter.[22] This opinion is re-echoed by Cocchi.[23] Vermeersch further states that unless the vicar or prefect had provided otherwise, upon their decease, the vicar delegate would succeed as pro-vicar or pro-prefect, if the Holy See had not made other arrangements. He bases his opinion upon the letters, "*Quam sublimi*" and "*Quam ex sublimi,*" of Benedict XIV already referred to. But in another work the same authority says that unless the vicar delegate were at the same time pro-vicar or pro-prefect as the case may be, "*sede vacante,*" the pro-vicar or pro-

21. Cfr. can. 197 §1.
22. Vermeersch, *Periodica* IX p. (25).
23. *Commentarium*, Lib. II, *De Personis*, p. 144.

prefect would rule, "*sede impedita,*" the vicar delegate.[24] The latter opinion is more in conformity with the canons referred to for guidance in the letter of Propaganda mentioned above, especially as it is stated therein "*eadem valeant quae de Vicario Generali in Codice I. C. statuta sunt*" (*can.* 366, *et seq.*). According to canon 371 the jurisdiction of the vicar general expires when the see is vacant, or the jurisdiction of the bishop is suspended. In conclusion then, it will suffice to restate that "*sede vacante*" the pro-vicar or pro-prefect rules, "*sede impedita*" the vicar delegate.

The rights and privileges of vicars delegate are to be determined, according to the direction of the letter of Propaganda, from a consideration of the canons affecting the status of vicars general. As often as the proper government of the mission demands, the Ordinary may freely appoint, as he may freely remove, a vicar delegate who will have ordinary jurisdiction in the whole territory. One only may be appointed unless a diversity of rites require more, though if the vicar delegate be absent or incapacitated, the vicar or prefect may temporarily appoint another in his place.[25]

The vicar delegate should be a member of the secular clergy, not less than thirty years of age, a doctor or licentiate of theology and Canon Law, or at least well versed in those branches, and commendable for sound doctrine, probity of life, prudence and experience.[26]

Where the vicariate or prefecture is entrusted to a religious order, the vicar delegate may be a member of that order.[27] This is not infrequently the case on many missions in the Far East.

It is also stipulated that the office of vicar delegate should not be assigned to a relative of the vicar or

---

24. *Epitome Juris Canonici*, vol. I, p. 144, n. 307.
25. Canon 366.
26. Canon 367 §1.
27. Canon 367 §2.

prefect, in the first or touching the first degree, nor to a pastor[28] or anyone having the care of souls, except in the case of necessity.[29]

By virtue of his office, the vicar delegate enjoys that spiritual and temporal jurisdiction in the whole mission, which the vicar or prefect has *iure ordinario*,[30] except what the latter reserves to himself, or which by law requires a special mandate from him.[31]

To exercise jurisdiction in the matters enumerated below a special mandate of the vicar or prefect is required, without which the vicar delegate cannot:

1. Excardinate or incardinate	canon	113
2. Confer ecclesiastical offices;	"	152
3. Convoke a synod;	"	357
4. Appoint pastors;[17]	"	455
5. Remove assistant priests;	"	477
6. Organize associations of the faithful;	"	686 §4
7. Reserve sins;	"	893
8. Grant dimissorial letters;	"	958
9. Permit marriages of conscience;	"	1104
10. Consecrate places;	"	1155
11. Grant permission to build a church;	"	1162
12. Proclaim relics as authentic;	"	1283
13. Confer benefices;	"	1432
14. Inflict ecclesiastical punishments;	"	2220 §2
15. Absolve from excommunication *in foro externo*, apostates, heretics and schismatics;	"	2314 §2

28. In vicariates and prefectures, quasi-pastors.
29. Canon 367 §3.
30. Canon 198.
31. Canon 368 §1.

If the vicar delegate has occasion to act in any of the matters just enumerated, he must make special mention of the mandate given him by the vicar or prefect.

Unless otherwise informed, the vicar delegate can be the executor of Apostolic rescripts sent to the vicar or prefect, or his predecessor in the administration of the mission. He also enjoys the habitual faculties granted to the Ordinary by the Holy See.[32]

Canon 369 requires the vicar delegate to refer the important affairs of the Curia to the Ordinary and inform him of what has been done, or is to be done, to safeguard discipline among the clergy and the people. In the exercise of his powers he should be careful not to act contrary to the will of the vicar or prefect. By virtue of Canon 44 §2, a favor asked of and refused by the vicar delegate cannot be asked of the vicar or prefect without mention being made of the refusal by the vicar delegate, otherwise the vicar's concession is null and void. A favor which was refused by the vicar or prefect cannot validly be granted by the vicar delegate even though mention is made of the previous refusal.

There seems to be some doubt as to whether or not the vicar delegate has the honorary privileges given to the vicar general in can. 370, according to which, the vicar general takes precedence over the clergy of the diocese both at public and private functions, even when the bishop is present . . . unless there be one present with the episcopal character and he himself is not a bishop. If the vicar general is a titular bishop, he has all their privileges of honor, if not, he has during his term of office the privileges and insignia of a titular protonotary apostolic.

Vermeersch is inclined to deny to vicars delegate these honorary rights: "*ideoque dicta de Vicario generali valent omnino pro Vicario Delegato; exceptis*

32. Canon 368 §2.

tamen privilegiis honorificiis de quibus adhuc desideratur declaratio S. Sedis."[33]

The letter of Dec. 9, 1919, authorizing their appointment, states that to vicars delegate: "*practice concessa sit jurisdictio in spiritualibus et temporalibus, qua ex Codice I. C. uti potest Vicarius Generalis in diocesi.*" While, therefore, they have practically all the jurisdiction of vicars general, a precise interpretation of the letter fails to afford any foundation for believing that they have their honorary privileges.

The question quite naturally arises, could not the vicar or prefect, even before the letter of Propaganda just mentioned, depute one of the priests, "*ad universitatem negotiorum,*" who could rightly be called their *delegatus?* Can. 199 §1 allows one with ordinary jurisdiction, hence a vicar or prefect, to delegate it in whole or in part unless it is expressly prohibited. The delegate who has, what may be termed, universal jurisdiction, may in turn sub-delegate in particular cases. While the faculties delegated to vicars and prefects by the Holy See may be sub-delegated to this "*delegatus*" further sub-delegation is expressly prohibited by can. 199 §5. Unless the power of jurisdiction was given "*ad beneplacitum nostrum*" the jurisdiction of a "*delegatus*" with universal jurisdiction (*ad universitatem negotiorum*) would not cease upon the death of the vicar or prefect.[34]

Canon 364 states that the appointment of the officials of the Curia, v. g. vicar general, the bishop's consultors, etc., must be made in writing,[35] and before entering upon their respective duties they must take an oath that they will: 1) faithfully discharge their office without respect of persons; 2) fulfill their

33. *Periodica* XII, p. (109).
34. Cfr. can. 207 §1.
writing.
36. Vermeersch, *Periodica,* XII p. (108).

respective duties under the authority of the bishop and according to the norms laid down in the canons; 3) observe secrecy within the limits and to the extent set by law or by the bishop.

While it is not correct to say that this canon is intended for vicars and prefects, by virtue of can. 294 §1 they have the same rights and faculties in their respective territories as bishops in their dioceses and therefore could require an oath such as described, from their vicar delegate and consultors. The wisdom of such a provision cannot easily be questioned. There would be scarcely any reason for the pro-vicar or the pro-prefect taking this oath unless he is at the same time, vicar delegate or one of the consultors.

There is no formula prescribed for this oath and possibly, therefore, the one given below may prove helpful:

Ego N. N., tacto pectore, praemissa divina nominis invocatione; iuro et promitto fideliter adimplere ad mentem Sacrorum Canonum, sine ulla exceptione personarum munus mihi commissum, circa . . .Et ita promitto et iuro; sic me Deus adiuvet.[36]

---

35. Can. 159 states that appointment to any office should be made in

PART II

Special Faculties Granted to Vicars and Prefects by the Congregation of Propaganda with a Commentary

Preamble

Many faculties which formerly vicars and prefects had only by special indult are now granted them by law as Ordinaries, since they are included in the terms, *Ordinarius* and *Ordinarius loci* of can. 198. The faculty for binating is treated in canon 806; canons 1532-1534 treat of the Ordinary's power to alienate church property; canon 1006 allows a bishop, hence a vicar apostolic, to confer major orders, for a serious reason, on any Sunday or holy day; canons 1043-1045 treat the Ordinary's power of dispensing in matrimonial cases, etc. In short, wherever the words *Ordinarius,* or *Ordinarius loci* are found in the Code, we may substitute for either vicar or prefect apostolic.

As regards the Ordinary's power of dispensing, there are several canons deserving of particular attention. Canon 15 states that laws, even those which are nullifying or disqualifying do not oblige in case of doubt which affects the law, i. e. "*in dubio iuris.*" If the doubt concerns a fact, "*in dubio facti,*" the Ordinary may dispense, provided the law is one from which the Roman Pontiff is accustomed to dispense.

This canon is referring to ecclesiastical laws only. *Ordinarius* includes all those mentioned in canon 198, par. 1, and hence vicars and prefects apostolic. The term Roman Pontiff is to be interpreted broadly and means also the Roman Congregations and Tribunals.

"In quibus Romanus Pontifex dispensare solet," hence this canon would be of no avail in the case of the two impediments mentioned in can. 1043, *"provenientibus ex sacro presbyteratus ordine et ex affinitate in linea recta, consummato matrimonio."* The above mentioned canon (no. 15) will be found very useful in matrimonial cases.

Ordinaries inferior to the Roman Pontiff cannot dispense from the general laws of the Church, not even in a particular case, unless this power has been granted to them implicitly or explicitly, or, when recourse to the Holy See is difficult and there is grave danger in delay and the dispensation requested is one which the Holy See usually grants.[1] Recourse to the Holy See must be difficult, not necessarily impossible. One would not be obliged to resort to the use of telephone, cable or airplane, as these are considered as extraordinary means of communication. Scandal or injury to one's reputation, would suffice to constitute a serious danger.[2] The dispensation must be one which the Holy See usually grants, e. g. from the impediment of consanguinity in the second or third degree, *lineae collateralis.* Besides the example from can. 1043 cited above, the Holy See rarely dispenses from the impediment of abduction.[3] The impediment of crime arising from adultery with the murder of the consort, or murder of the consort as the result of the plotting of both accomplices, are cases which Wernz maintains the Church has never dispensed, nor is it inclined to do so when the murder is public.[4]

Ordinaries may dispense from diocesan laws absolutely, but from those of provincial and plenary councils, only according to the norm of can. 291 §2, viz., in individual cases and for a just cause. Furthermore they cannot dispense from laws given by the Roman

---

1. Canon 81.
2. Augustine, Commentary, II, p. 177.
3. Gasparri, *Tractatus Canonicus de Matrimonio*, n. 649.
4. Wernz, *Ius Matrimoniale* (Lib. IV, Ius Decr.), n. 534; cfr. also Gasparri, *Tractatus Canonicus de Matrimonio*, n. 743.

Pontiff, especially for that particular diocese or territory, except in the instance mentioned in can. 81.[5]

On January 1, 1920, the new faculties which had been approved on Feb. 6. 1919, by the late Pope Benedict XV, became effective for vicars and prefects apostolic. At the same time all other faculties granted by the Congregation of Propaganda were abrogated as having expired on the thirty-first of December, 1919.[6] There are now three formulas, *Formula Prima, Secunda* and *Tertia.* They are no longer distinguished as ordinary and extraordinary but as *maior* and *minor.* The *formulae maiores* are intended for those with the episcopal character, the *formulae minores* are for the other mission superiors.

Formula I is for Sweden, Norway, Denmark, Smyrna, Constantinople, Jerusalem, the Mesopotamian district and Arabia (vicariate apostolic), Tripoli, Egypt and Morocco. Formula II is for Tasmania, Wellington (New Zealand), the West Indies and dioceses of Central America, and the dioceses in the French and English colonies of Africa. Formula III takes in China and Japan, the Oceanic Islands, Africa, except Tripoli, Egypt and the French dioceses, India, Malacca, and the vicariates and prefectures of America.[7]

General Rules of Interpretation

Habitual faculties are considered as *privilegia praeter ius* and are those granted *in perpetuum,* or for a certain length of time, or for a definite number of cases.[8] What number of cases would suffice? *Salvo meliori iudicio,* two are sufficient.

---

5. Canon 82.
6. Vermeersch, *De Formulis Facultatum S. C. de Propaganda Fide, Periodica* XI, p. (70).
7. Vermeersch, *De F. F. Periodica,* XI, p. (71).
8. Canon 66 §1.

Privileges are to be interpreted according to their meaning and must neither be restricted nor extended.[9] The faculty of dispensing granted for a particular case is subject to strict interpretation,[10] i. e. it may not be applied to any other person or persons than those for whom the faculty was specifically granted.

Unless granted for personal reasons or otherwise provided by law habitual faculties are not withdrawn nor do they automatically cease with the cessation of the authority of the Ordinary to whom they were granted by the Holy See,[11] but the faculties persist in favor of the administrator of the vicariate or prefecture who would be the pro-vicar or pro-prefect or, in the case mentioned in can. 309 §4, the senior priest.

Faculties carry with them the right to use all the means necessary for their exercise. Hence the faculty of dispensing includes the power to absolve from censures but only for the purpose of rendering the subject capable of receiving the dispensation.[12]

Even when there is a doubt as to the sufficiency of the cause, a dispensation may be lawfully asked for and both licitly and validly granted.[13]

Faculties are given for the external forum, for the internal, and for the internal sacramental forum. An act of jurisdiction in the external forum, whether ordinary or delegated, holds also for the internal forum, but not *vice versa*.[14]

The executor of a rescript who has made a mistake in its execution must execute it again.[15] The reason is clear, if he erred and acted invalidly, the rescript was never executed. Unless there was a prohibition or some

9. Canon 67.
10. Canon 85.
11. Canon 66 §2.
12. Canon 66 §3.
13. Canon 84 §2.
14. Canon 202 §1.
15. Canon 59 §1.

particular person was designated, the executor may appoint a substitute.[16]

Jurisdiction granted for the internal forum is still validly exercised even if through oversight, the priest has failed to notice that the time for his faculties has expired or that he had used up the number of cases allowed by the faculty.[17]

"*Gratia gratiam non impedit,*" wherefore, unless the clause, "*dummodo nulla altera existat vel concessa fuerit,*" or a simpler restriction were imposed, two faculties could coalesce. An example of a prohibitory clause is found in can. 916 which gives bishops, abbots, etc., the right to declare daily privileged forever, one altar in their cathedral, abbatial, etc. church, "*dummodo aliud non habeatur.*"[18]

Conditions imposed in rescripts are not required for validity except when they are expressed by the particles "*si,*" "*dummodo*" or others expressing a like signification.[19] There seems to be a little doubt about the ablative absolute. Even before the Code such an eminent authority as d'Annibale only dubiously proposed it as expressing a condition "*ad valorem.*"[20] Vermeersch,[21] against Maroto,[22] maintains that the ablative absolute does not express a condition for validity. From the words of the canon, "*vel aliam eiusdem significationis*" it is evident that all the conditions "*ad validitatem*" are not contained therein.

Jurisdiction delegated by the Holy See can be sub-delegated either for one act or habitually. But sub-delegated jurisdiction cannot be further sub-delegated unless this power has been expressly granted.[23] In prac-

16. Canon 57.
17. Canon 207 §2.
18. Vermeersch, *Periodica* XI, p. (74) n. 40.
19. Canon 39.
20. D'Annibale, *Summa Theologiae Moralis*, I, 76; III, 500 & 502.
21. *Epitome Juris Canonici*, I, n. 114.
22. *Institutiones Iuris Canonici*, I, n. 284.
23. Canon 199 §5.

tice, therefore, those faculties which have been granted to the Ordinary as communicable can be given to the missionaries for a single case or habitually, but neither vicars nor prefects apostolic nor their vicars delegate can give the missionaries power of further sub-delegation.

Non-judicial or voluntary jurisdiction may be used in one's own favor and outside of one's territory unless the nature of the case or the law itself forbid such use of jurisdiction.[24] Thus one who has the necessary faculties could dispense himself from fasting. Voluntary jurisdiction may be exercised in favor of a subject outside of one's territory even when both superior and subject are outside of the territory.

Special Rules of Interpretation

At the end of the formulas there are a few observations explaining their use.

1. Only those faculties marked with an asterisk may be sub-delegated. Consequently those without the asterisk may be exercised only by the vicar or prefect apostolic and their vicars delegate.

2. The Ordinary, whether *per se* or *per alios*, can exercise the faculties validly only within the confines of his jurisdiction. Canon 201 clearly distinguishes between those acts of jurisdiction which may be exercised outside of, and those which may be exercised only within one's territory. The clause, "*infra fines suae jurisdictionis,*" is to be interpreted in the light of this canon. Wherefore the Ordinary may grant sacramental absolution to his subjects everywhere, but in the exercise of faculties requiring judicial jurisdiction, the Ordinary is restricted to his own territory except in the case mentioned in can. 201 §2.

24. Canon 201 §3.

By its very nature the faculty of declaring altars privileged, is restricted to one's own territory and the same may be said of the faculty for erecting the Stations of the Cross or of any others whose effects are purely local.

3. The faculties are to be exercised gratuitously. However, it would not be forbidden to charge a small sum to cover chancery expenses or mailing costs.[25]

4. Mention must be made of the Apostolic delegation. Canon 1057 requires this for matrimonial dispensations. Here the reference is to the Ordinary, whether exercising the faculties himself or sub-delegating them to the missionaries.

The prescriptions that the faculties be exercised gratuitously and that mention be made of the Apostolic delegation, affect only their licit use.

De Tempore a quo et ad quod

"Quod si forte ex oblivione vel inadvertentia ultra tempus supra praefinitum . . . hisce facultatibus Ordinarium uti contingat, absolutiones, dispensationes, concessiones, omnes exinde impertitae uti ratae atque validae habeantur. Insuper datis ab Ordinario precibus pro renovatione seu prorogatione earundem facultatum, ipsae in suo robore perseverare censeantur usque dum responsum S. C. ad eundem Ordinarium pervenerit."

From this it will be seen that whereas for jurisdiction exercised through inadvertence in excess of the time or number of cases prescribed in the faculty, canon 207 §2 supplies jurisdiction only for the internal forum; the faculties of vicars and prefects extend this power to the external forum.

The word "*facultatum*" includes, without exception, everything contained in the formulas. While the *use*

25. Cfr. can. 1056 on matrimonial dispensations.

of the faculties after the expiration of the fixed time, or when the number of cases has been exhausted, may be either on the part of the Ordinary or a sub-delegate, the oversight or inadvertency must be on the part of the Ordinary. For example, through inadvertency, the Ordinary has granted one of the missionaries the faculty of dispensing from an impediment after his faculties have expired. In this case the missionary validly dispenses, but not in the case when he makes use of the dispensation after the expiration of the time set by the Ordinary.

"Insuper, datis ab Ordinario precibus pro renovatione seu prorogatione earundem facultatum, ipsae in suo robore perseverare censeantur usque dum responsum S. C. ad eundem Ordinarium pervenerit."

It may frequently happen that letters are delayed, especially when they are directed to countries where the conditions are very unsettled. In the event of a delay the Ordinary need not be concerned as his faculties perdure. Supposing that he had received a faculty to dispense in ten cases from the impediment of age, and before the number was exhausted, he applied for a renewal of the faculty. Even if in the meantime the number allowed him had been used up and another case occurred; he could dispense and then count it as number one of the new grant.[26] If the Holy See should renew the faculty, the validity of the dispensation would be questioned by no one. But even if the Holy See should deny the renewal of the faculty, the dispensation given would certainly be valid since it is expressly stated: *"ipsae (facultates) in suo robore perseverare censeantur usque dum responsum S. C. ad eundem Ordinarium pervenerit."* In fine, the validity of such a dispensation is provided for without regard to the character of the forthcoming response of the Holy See.

26. Vermeersch, *Periodica*, XI, p. (80).

From what moment is the time for which the faculties are given, to be reckoned? On two occasions in answer to this question, the Sacred Congregation of Propaganda replied that the time was to be reckoned from the day they were received.[27] In practice, any prescriptions of the Holy See on the matter must be observed. But if there are no provisions given, the *tempus a quo* may be reckoned according to the rule given by Propaganda, viz., from the day of reception. Concerning the calculation of time, can. 34 §3 states that when the *tempus a quo* does not coincide with the beginning of the day, the first day being incomplete, is not counted, and the time expires when the last day of the same number is ended. If, therefore, the formula were received sometime on the twenty-second of February, 1920, and was given *ad decennium,* the time would elapse at midnight on the twenty-second of February, 1930.

FORMULA TERTIA MINOR.

A. Circa Sacramenta et Ritus Sacros.

1. Concedendi suis missionariis facultatem *benedicendi aquam baptismalem* ea breviori formula, qua Missionariis Peruanis apud Indos Summus Pontifex Paulus III uti concessit.

Except in the cases given in can. 759, baptism should be conferred solemnly and water blessed for that purpose should be used.[28] When the supply is exhausted or the water has become putrid, fresh water should be put into the font and blessed as prescribed by the Ritual,[29] *Tit.* II, *Cap.* 7, "*Benedictio Fontis Baptismi extra Sabbatum Paschae et Pentecostes.*"

The Faculty. Instead of the longer form for the blessing of the font outside of Holy Saturday and the

27. S. C. P. F. 2 April, 1640—*Collectanea S. C. P. F.* n. 100; 22 Jan. 1759—*Collectanea*, S. C. P. F. n. 412.
28. Canons 755 §1 & 757 §1, 2.

Vigil of Pentecost, the faculty permits the use of a very short form consisting of two prayers which may be found on the first page of the appendix to the *Rituale Romanum.* The faculty may be given by the Ordinary to all the missionaries or priests who are engaged in the sacred ministry in his territory, even to those who are only temporarily there.

2. Concedendi facultatem *administrandi Confirmationis Sacramentum* uni vel alteri ex suis sacerdotibus, in quacumque regione a sua residentia longe dissita, absente tamen quocumque Episcopo, servato Decreto Sacrae huius Congreg. diei 4 maii anni 1774, atque Instructione "De Sacramento Confirmationis" in appendice Ritualis Romani inserta.

According to can. 782, §3, vicars and prefects may confer the Sacrament of Confirmation, but only within the limits of their own territory and during their tenure of office. Since every consecrated bishop is the ordinary minister of Confirmation and can validly administer it everywhere the canon just referred to, is intended only for those vicars and prefects without the episcopal character.

The Faculty. The Ordinary can permit one or two of his priests, *i. e.*, missionaries to administer Confirmation under the conditions expressed in the faculty. "*Uni vel alteri.*" Is the number to be restricted to two only? Commentators upon the Apostolic faculties, are of the opinion that "*uni vel alteri*" means to a few, depending in number upon the size of the mission and the number of faithful.[30]

"*In quacumque regione a sua residentia dissita.*" The region may be distant because of the difficulty of access. The frequency of the journeys the Ordinary would otherwise be called upon to make, the loss of time occasioned by irregular and uncertain travelling facili-

---

29. Canon 755 §3.

30. Vermeersch, *Periodica,* XI, p. (113); Iglesias, *Brevis Commentarius in Facultates,* p. 33.

ties; these and innumerable other reasons would make it difficult and inadvisable for the Ordinary to do all the confirming himself.

"*Absente tamen quocumque Episcopo.*" This means that for the licit use of the faculty, the extraordinary minister should not avail himself of the faculty when a bishop, the ordinary minister of the Sacrament, is present and is both able and willing. If a bishop were present but either physically unable or unwilling, v. g., a neighboring bishop passing through the mission, the priest so empowered could lawfully make use of the faculty.

None of the conditions expressed are required "*ad validitatem*" inasmuch as they are not introduced by the particles "*si*" or "*dummodo*" which, as can. 39 states, express conditions "*ad validitatem.*"

The Decree and the Instruction referred to, together with the rite when the Sacrament is administered by a priest, are to be found in the "*Appendix ad Rituale Romanum*" under the title, "*De Sacramento Confirmationis.*"

3. Permittendi suis missionariis ut *Missam* celebrare possint, in casu necessitatis, etiam *sine ministro, sub dio* et *sub terra,* atque etiam *in mari,* dummodo mare sit tranquillum, in loco tamen decenti; etiam si altare sit fractum vel sine Reliquiis Sanctorum; et praesentibus hereticis, schismaticis, infidelibus et excommunicatis, si aliter celebrari non possit; atque ut Missa celebrari queat *una hora post mediam noctem.*

This faculty dispenses with several of the liturgical laws. It is to be granted by the Ordinary and may be given to any or all of his priests, even to those of his subjects who are absent.

"*In casu necessitatis,*" v. g. when otherwise one would be obliged to omit the celebration of Mass, or it may be interpreted thus, it is not lawful to make use of the faculty when all the customary requisites for the saying of Mass are present.[31]

"*Etiam sine ministro.* According to a decision of the Congregation of Rites, when the priest says Mass without a server, the *Confiteor* is said only once.[32] The "*vobis fratres*" and "*vos fratres*" may be omitted,[33] and in the "*Misereatur*" in place of "*vestri,*" the priest says "*nostri.*"[34] In the "*Suscipiat,*" in place of "*manibus tuis,*" he says "*manibus meis.*"[35] The priest must make all the responses which the server would make.

"*Sub dio et sub terra.*" Mass may be said in the open or "*sub terra,*" i. e. in times of persecution it might be necessary to resort to caves and under ground tunnels. As far as possible, care should be taken to choose a place suited to the sacredness of the function.

"*Atque etiam in mari dummodo mare sit tranquillum.*" During a storm or tempest at sea this faculty cannot be used. As a matter of fact the sea is often rough when there is no storm and therefore the use of the faculty on shipboard is to be determined according to the danger of spilling the Sacred Species.

"*In loco tamen decenti.*" A decree of the Congregation of Propaganda under date of March 1, 1902,[36] prohibited the use of private cabins of passengers for the celebration of Mass. Later that same year, in a letter to the vicar apostolic of Madagascar, dated August 13th,[37] the severity of the decree was somewhat mitigated. The Sacred Congregation declared that it wished to obviate abuses which might arise were Mass celebrated in private staterooms. However, it had not intended an

---

31. Iglesias, *Brevis Commentarius*, p. 36.
32. *S. R. C. in Erien.* 4 Sept. 1875—*Decreta authentica*, n. 3368.
33. Kunz, *Die liturgischen Verrichtungen des Celebranten, Theil I, Art.* I, n. 5 footnote, quoted by the Eccl. Rev. XXXVII, 657.
34. Cappello, *De Sacramentis*, I, n. 741.
35. *Ritus servandus in celebratione Missae*, VII, 7.
36. Decr. S. C. P. F. 1 March, 1902—*Collectanea* S. C. P. F. n. 2130.
37. *Collectanea S. C. P. F.* II, p. 424, footnote.

absolute prohibition and if all danger of irreverence was removed Mass would be permitted even in the staterooms. Priests were urged to find the most suitable place possible and in the absence of a more fitting place, the stateroom could be utilized.

Canon 822 §4 states that the Ordinary can give permission for a just and reasonable cause to celebrate Holy Mass outside a church or oratory on a consecrated stone, in a decent place, *but never in a bedroom.* However, the Congregation of Propaganda did give permission to say Mass in the sleeping room of a sick person when there was no other way of administering Viaticum.[38] The same permission was granted in order that the faithful might fulfill the precept of paschal communion. The priest was to see that there were no indecent or superstitious emblems in the room.[39]

Canon 823 §1 forbids the celebration of Mass in the churches of heretics and schismatics, even though these may have been once properly consecrated or blessed. Such an act may easily be construed as an approval of false worship. However, there have been cases of necessity when such permissions have been given. The Holy Office permitted Mass to be celebrated in a garrison chapel at Malacca in which Protestant services were also held,[40] and also permitted the use of churches in which both Catholics and Protestants held services, but at different hours.[41]

"Etiamsi altare sit fractum vel sine reliquiis Sanctorum." The faculty allows the celebration of Mass in those circumstances forbidden by canon 1200, viz., when the altar stone has lost its consecration by either the

38. S. C. P. F. 6 Sept. 1821—*Collectanea S. C. P. F.* n. 764.

39. S. C. P. F. 6 Sept. 1821—*Collectanea* n. 764 Cfr. S. C. P. F. 14 Dec. 1668, *Coll.* n. 172; 17 April, 1758—*Coll.* 411 ad 4.

40. *S. C. S. Off.* 5 June, 1889—*Collectanea S. C. P. F.* n. 1707.

41. S. C. S. Off. 13 June, 1634—*Collectanea S. C. P. F.* n. 75; Cfr. Konings-Putzer, *Commentarium in Facultates Apostolicas,* p. 279.

removal of the relics, or because of a considerable break in the stone.

"Praesentibus haereticis, schismaticis, infidelibus, et excommunicatis." The celebration of Mass before any of the above is not forbidden by law unless there be one present who is an *"excommunicatus vitandus."* In this event, according to can. 2259, §2, he must be expelled and if this cannot be done, the Mass must be stopped if it can be done without great inconvenience. The faculty allows the priest in case of necessity to celebrate Mass even though there be an *"excommunicatus vitandus"* among those present.

"Atque ut Missa celebrari queat una hora post mediam noctem." The Code in can. 821 §1 states that Mass should not begin earlier than one hour before daybreak. The celebration of Mass one hour after midnight requires that there be some necessity for doing so. A reason sufficient to justify the use of this faculty would be the desire to get an early start on a journey so as to avoid the heat of the midday sun.

4. Permittendi ut *Missa celebrari* possit *cum uno luminari*, adhibendo casu quodcumque lumen, dummodo cera ex apum industria confectum deficiat; nec non permittendi ut Missa *absque luminaribus celebrari* possit, in locis ubi non inveniuntur olivae et nulla alia substantia ad lampades nutriendas inveniri potest: in casu tamen verae necessitatis, et graviter onerata conscientia ipsius Ordinarii.

The rubrics of the Mass prescribe that two beeswax candles be kept burning on the altar during Mass.[42] To say Mass without any lighted candles would be a grave sin, with one only a venial sin, except, however, in case of necessity, e. g. when Viaticum is to be administered.[43]

The faculty permits the celebration of Mass with one light of any substance, provided that there be no beeswax available. There is question here only of moral

---

42. *Rubricae gen. missae*, n. 44.
43. Noldin, *De Sacramentis* p. 248, n. 211.

impossibility and if the cost of beeswax were prohibitive or if it were difficult to obtain, the faculty could be used.

When olive oil or any other substance suitable for lighting purposes cannot be obtained and in case of necessity "*graviter onerata conscientia Ordinarii,*" Mass is permitted without any light whatsoever.

5. Permittendi ut in utraque *purificatione calicis aqua tantum* adhiberi possit, dummodo tamen extrema adsit vini deficientia.

After consuming the Precious Blood, the rubrics prescribe that wine only be taken for the first ablution, for the second, both wine and water. A priest would be guilty of a venial sin were he to use water only for both ablutions, according to the teaching of St. Alphonsus.[44]

The faculty permits the use of water for both ablutions, "*Dummodo extrema adsit vini deficientia.*" Note that the faculty concerns only the lack of wine and not the necessity of saying Mass, wherefore if the supply of wine were very low, the priest could say Mass *sola ex devotione* and yet make use of this concession.

6. Permittendi *thurificationem* in Missis cantatis a solo celebrante absque ministris, dummodo duo saltem clerici superpelliceo induti Missae inserviant.

No deacon or sub-deacon is required and the Mass is the regular *missa cantata*. "*Duo clerici superpelliceo induti,*" i. e. two boys who know how to serve Mass not necessarily two clerics in the strictly canonical sense. Only two are required although the services of a third as thurifer would add greatly to the dignity of the occasion. By its very nature the use of this faculty is restricted to the territory of the Ordinary.

7. Permittendi ut in Ecclesiis sui territorii *tres* Missae statim post mediam noctem *Nativitatis Domini* celebrari possint, cum potestate administrandi fidelibus S. Communionem, cauto tamen ut omnia cum debita reverentia fiant.

---

44. St. Alphonsus, *Lib. V, cap. III*, n. 408.

Canon 821 §2 states that on Christmas Day only the conventual or parochial Mass may be begun at midnight, but no other except by Apostolic indult. There seems to be a doubt in the minds of some as to whether Holy Communion may be given at this midnight Mass without special permission. The authors now hold that whenever Mass is permitted, Holy Communion may be distributed.[45]

Canon 821 §3 states that in all religious or pious houses having an oratory with the right of reserving the Blessed Sacrament, one priest may at midnight, Christmas, say one or three Masses and those who assist will satisfy their obligation of hearing Mass, and Holy Communion may be distributed to those who wish to receive.

By virtue of the faculty the Ordinary may permit three Masses to be celebrated at midnight Christmas in all the churches, and Holy Communion may be distributed at all of the Masses.[46]

"*In Ecclesiis,*" and therefore in public oratories, which, according to can. 1191 §1, are governed by the same laws as churches. Canon 821 §2 allows a pastor or quasi-pastor to say one parochial Mass at midnight Christmas Day while §3 of the same canon states that in all religious houses having an oratory with the right of keeping there habitually the Blessed Sacrament, one priest may at midnight Christmas say one or also the three Masses. Supposing that the pastor or quasi-pastor, or the priest mentioned in §3 wishes to avail himself of the permission given by the law to celebrate one Mass at midnight, would this Mass in any way prevent the celebration of the three Masses (by another priest) as granted by the faculty? There is certainly no prohibition in the faculty itself and one may feel secure in the rule

45. Vermeersch, *Epitome,* II, p. 50, n. 97; Iglesias, *Brevis Commentarius*. p. 41, footnote.

46. Cfr. canons 846 §1 & 867 §4.

already cited, "*gratia gratiam non impedit,*" and say that the Mass allowed by the above mentioned canon may be permitted together with those conceded by the faculty.

The admonition that due reverence be observed demands that those who plan to receive Holy Communion should prepare themselves for a worthy reception of the Eucharist. To this end the Ordinary is free to lay down any precepts that he deems necessary.

8. Permittendi ut in Ecclesiis sui territorii *functiones Maioris Hebdomadae* celebrari valeant iuxta peculiarem ritum a S. M. Benedicto PP. XIII propositum pro Ecclesiis minoribus paroecialibus, in quibus ministrorum numerus vel copia cantorum ad praedictam sacras functiones solemniter peragendas haberi nequeat, dummodo tamen constet ibidem satis esse consultum reverentiae sacris mysteriis debitae, et quod nulla exinde abusui pateat occasio; et quatenus neque praedictus ritus servari possit, permittendi ut in iisdem Ecclesiis unica Missa lecta loco solemnis, celebrari possit feria V in Coena Domini et Sabbato Sancto.

Whenever possible, the functions of Holy Week are to be carried out in detail and in the manner prescribed in the Missal. With the permission of the bishop, in parishes where this is impossible, they must be conducted without the chant and in the manner described in the rite of Benedict XIII.[47] What is permitted *iure communi* in the parish churches is extended by the faculty to all the churches in the territory of the Ordinary. Furthermore, where the functions cannot be carried out in detail, he may permit a low Mass to be said on Holy Thursday and Holy Saturday instead of the customary solemn Mass.

For the more simple form according to the rite of Benedict XIII, at least three altar boys are necessary

---

47. The *Memoriale Rituum* of Benedict XIII gives directions for the Holy Week ceremonies where there are no ministers, i. e. deacon and subdeacon. It was published in 1725 for the convenience of the smaller parish churches in Rome. Later, in 1821, Pius VI extended its use to all small churches of the Roman Rite.

and all the ceremonies should be carried out with the proper decorum so that there will be no opportunity for abuses to arise.[48] In passing, it is worth noting that since permission has been granted in the faculty for a low Mass on Thursday and Saturday of Holy Week, Communion may be distributed. But on the latter day, as can. 867 §3 states, it may be given only during Mass or immediately after it.

9. Permittendi ut in Ecclesiis sui territorii ter in hebdomada, extra Quadragesimam, *Missa privata de requie* celebrari possit, etiam diebus ritus duplicis maioris et minoris, exceptis Dominicis, nec non feriis, vigiliis atque octavis privilegiatis, diebus tamen, quibus eadem Missa a Rubricis permittitur, computatis.

This faculty allows the celebration of three private requiem Masses each week in all the churches of the vicariate or prefecture, even on those days which, according to the calendar, are greater or lesser doubles. The exceptions to the use of this faculty are as follows: during Lent and on Sundays, on privileged octaves, vigils and ferials.

The privileged ferials are those of Ash Wednesday, and Holy Week; the privileged vigils, those of Christmas, Epiphany and Pentecost; the privileged octaves, those of Easter, Pentecost, Epiphany, Corpus Christi, Christmas and the Ascension.

"Diebus tamen quibus eadem Missa a Rubricis permittitur, computatis." This is a local indult, hence if three semi-doubles occur during a week, a requiem cannot be celebrated on the three remaining days which are doubles. If only one semi-double occurs during the week, two doubles may be selected for the second and third requiem. If this indult were personal, the quasi-pastor could select Monday, Tuesday and Wednesday, and his assistant could take Thursday, Friday and

48. *Memoriale Rituum*, cfr. *Monitum*.

Saturday, that is, were every day of a week a double. and therefore, with the exception of the days noted in the faculty, a requiem Mass could be celebrated on every day of the year. But there is no reason to believe that the faculty grants such a privilege and therefore, if every day of the week be a double, three of these may be selected and on these days the quasi-pastor and his assistants must say the requiem Mass if they wish to make use of the faculty.[49]

10. Permittendi etiam omnibus diebus festis et dominicis *Missam votivam de B. M. V.* iis qui, ob defectum oculorum aliamve infirmitatem, legere nequeant Missas singulis diebus occurrentes iuxta Missalis Romani rubricas.

The Ordinary may permit a priest whose sight is failing or who is suffering from some infirmity, e. g. such a defect of speech as stammering, to say daily the votive Mass of the Blessed Virgin. The fact that a priest enjoys this indult does not prevent him in the least from saying a requiem Mass when the rubrics permit and he may also say the Mass of the day when he so desires.

An Instruction of the Congregation of Rites, January 12, 1921,[50] gives all the points to be observed by a priest who enjoys such an indult as the one described above. The three orations, the *Gloria* and *Credo* are to be said when the rubrics prescribe. On Christmas Day the priest is to say the votive Mass three times while on All Souls' Day, he says the *Missa quotidiana defunctorum* three times. The other points mentioned in the Instruction may be found in the *"Acta Apostolicae Sedis," XIII*, 154.

11. Permittendi ut, iusta de causa, *Ssmum Sacramentum cum duobus luminaribus* ex quacumque substantia confectis *exponi* possit.

49. Cfr. Eccl. Rev. XL, 230.
50. *A. A. S. XIII*, 154.

For the exposition of the Blessed Sacrament at least six candles are necessary; for exposition during Forty Hours, at least twenty.[51]

By virtue of this faculty the Ordinary may permit the exposition whether public or private, with only two lights on the altar. These lights may be of any substance whatever and commentators are inclined to permit the use of electric light.[52]

A just cause is required for the licit use of this faculty. Such would be the prohibitive cost of wax candles or the moral impossibility of obtaining them. It is to be noted that the above faculty is intended only for the exposition of the Blessed Sacrament, i. e. for Benediction, and not for the celebration of Mass, or for the reservation of the Bl. Sacrament.[53] Blat thinks that it may not be used for the Forty Hours devotion,[54] but this would seem to frustrate one of the ends for which the faculty was intended.

12. Permittendi ut, in locis ubi olivae non inveniuntur, et nulla alia substantia ad lampades nutriendas haberi potest *Sanctissimum Sacramentum* etiam *sine lumine asservari* possit, in casu tamen verae necessitatis et graviter onerata conscientia ipsius Ordinarii.

Canon 1271 states that before the tabernacle in which the Bl. Sacrament is kept, there should burn at least one lamp day and night, fed either with olive oil or beeswax. Where olive oil is not easily obtainable, the Ordinary, according to his prudent judgment, may allow the use of other oils which, as far as possible, should be vegetable oils.

---

51. *S. R. C.* 15 March, 1698, *Decreta authentica*, n. 1992; De Herdt, *S. Liturgiae Praxis*, I, p. 253 n. 184 ad 4.

52. Vermeersch, *Periodica*, XI, p. (116); Iglesias, *Brevis Commentarius*, p. 48.

53. Vermeersch, *Periodica*, XI, p. (117).

54. Blat, *Commentarium Iuris Canonici*, *III*, pars I, p. 722.

All the authors understand the obligation of keeping a lamp burning before the Bl. Sacrament, to bind *sub gravi*.[55]

The faculty postulates a condition where neither olive oil or any other substance suitable as fuel for the lamp is available and under these circumstances the Ordinary may permit the Bl. Sacrament to be kept without any light whatsoever, "*in casu tamen verae necessitatis et graviter onerata conscientia Ordinarii.*"

One commentator upon this faculty maintains that there is a "*vera necessitas*" for reserving the Blessed Sacrament in those churches having the care of souls and where, as stated in can. 1265 §1 n. 1, it must be kept by law. Among the places referred to are quasi-parishes, and churches attached to houses of exempt religious. The reason he assigns for the necessity, is the obligation of administering Viaticum which, as theologians commonly hold, is "*iure divino*."[56] Another reason sufficiently grave to warrant the use of this faculty would be the deprivation of the spiritual comfort of a visit to the Blessed Sacrament which otherwise the people, or a religious community would have to suffer.

13. Permittendi, si ab hereticis aut infidelibus sit periculum sacrilegii ut *Ssmum Sacramentum* pro infirmis *sine lumine* in loco tamen decenti *retineri* possit.

The preceding faculty presumes a condition when it is morally impossible to secure the required fuel for the sanctuary lamp. The present faculty, however, is not concerned with a lack of fuel, but treats of the place where the Blessed Sacrament may be kept when there is danger of sacrilege at the hands of heretics or infidels.

According to the Code, the Blessed Sacrament must be kept in an irremovable tabernacle placed in the middle

---

55. St. Alph. *Lib. V. cap.* III, p. 315; Cappello, I, p. 277, n. 401; Vermeersch *Periodica*, XI p. (134).

56. Iglesias, *Brevis Commentarius*, p. 50.

of the altar. For a grave reason and with the permission of the Ordinary it is permissible to remove the Blessed Sacrament from the tabernacle over night and keep it in a more secure, but decent place, on a corporal and with a light burning before it.[57]

The faculty permits the Blessed Sacrament to be reserved in a place other than that required by can. 1269 mentioned above. The choice of a *"locus decens"* is left to the priest. An empty room or closet would do well, but closets used for storage purposes, the drawers of a table, chiffonier, etc., or the pocket of an overcoat should never be utilized as a repository for the Blessed Sacrament. As long as the danger exists, the faculty may be used, but if the danger is present only at night, the Blessed Sacrament must be restored to its customary place in the morning.

The faculty dispenses from the law requiring the tabernacle lamp. Commentators, however, are inclined to insist that a light be kept burning, when the circumstances are such that all danger of irreverence or sacrilege is removed by the transfer of the Blessed Sacrament from the altar.[58]

The purpose of the faculty permitting the reservation of the Blessed Sacrament under these unusual conditions, is to have Viaticum and Holy Communion for the sick.

*14. Permittendi *religiosis sororibus* sacrarii servitio addictis ut vasa sacrasque supellectiles tangere, nec non pallas, *corporalia et purificatoria abluere* valeant.

Care must be taken that the chalice and paten and unwashed purificators, palls and corporals are not touched except by clerics or those who have the care of such. The purificators, palls and corporals used at Mass shall not be given to lay persons nor even to religious

57. Canon 1269.

58. Konings-Putzer, *Commentarium in Facultates Apostolicas*, edit. 1897, p. 288, n. 165.

to be washed until they have first been washed by a cleric in major orders. The water of the first washing should be poured into the sacrarium or, if there be none, into the fire.[59]

Since this faculty is marked with an asterisk, the Ordinary may sub-delegate it to the missionaries. The permission given in the canon cited above, is intended only for those who have charge of the sacristy, and under this head would come Sister sacristans. But certainly the faculty intends to give more than what is granted *iure communi*, and so it would seem that the Sister to whom the faculty grants permission to handle the sacred vessels, etc., should be understood in a broader sense in the faculty than in the canon referred to above. The latter requires that she have charge of the sacred vessels "*qui eorum custodiam habent.*" For the use of the faculty it would probably suffice that she be more or less connected with the sacristy.

Canon 1306 §2 states that the purificators, palls and corporals be first washed by a cleric in sacred orders, but the faculty permits even the first washing to be done by the Sisters. They, too, should pour the water from the first washing into the sacrarium or into the fire.

15. Permittendi suis missionariis ut *administrare* valeant christianis graviter decumbentibus *Ssmam Eucharistiam sine lumine* et sine superpelliceo et stola, dummodo constet de periculo cui exponerentur si induerent superpelliceum et stolam, lumenve accenderetur.

Holy Communion should be brought publicly to the sick unless there are good reasons which make the private ministration advisable.[60] Public ministration means that the priest is accompanied by some of the faithful or by a cleric or a layman who carries a light.[61]

---

59. Canon 1306 §1.
60. Canon 847.
61. *Rituale Romanum, Tit. IV, cap. IV, De communione infirmorum,* n. 10.

As we have just seen, the Code permits Holy Communion to be brought privately to the sick when there is a reasonable cause. The priest must wear a stole under his coat and the pyx must be placed in a burse carried on the breast and suspended by strings from the neck. The priest should never go alone but should take at least one companion along.[62]

The faculty, however, is not concerned with the bringing of Holy Communion, but with its administration. By virtue of the faculty, the Ordinary can permit the missionaries to administer Holy Communion to those gravely ill, without any light whatsoever and without either the surplice or stole prescribed by the liturgy. The use of the faculty is not merely confined to the administration of viaticum but is intended also for the giving of Communion of devotion. This is evident from the text which uses the words, "*Ssmam Eucharistiam.*"

"*Graviter decumbentibus*" are those who are very sick with a disease or ailment that is likely to become dangerous or terminate fatally.

"*Dummodo constet de periculo,*" etc. This clause is necessary for the valid use of the faculty. The danger may be either to the sick person or to the priest. If all danger is removed by dispensing with the candles or lights, the surplice and stole should be worn and *vice versa.*[63]

*16. Concedendi *infirmis decumbentibus,* de quibus certa spes non adsit ut cito convalescant, etiam ante finem mensis, a quo decumbunt, ut *S. Communionem* sumere possint bis vel ter in hebdomada; et si agatur de sacerdotibus vel religiosis, etiam quotidie, *non servato ieiunio*: hoc est etsi aliquam medicinam vel aliquid per modum potus antea sumpserint.

This is a faculty which can be sub-delegated. It is an amplification of can. 858 §2, both in respect to time

62. *Rituale Romanum, Tit.* IV, *cap,* IV, *De communione infirmorum,* n. 10.

63. Vermeersch, *Periodica* XI, p. (136).

and to the number of communions. The faculty omits the "*qui iam a mense decumbunt*" of the canon and it suffices that there be no hope of an immediate recovery, "*ut cito convalescat,*" which being interpreted means within three or four days.[64] The canon permits Holy Communion once or twice a week, to one not fasting, whereas the faculty allows Communion two or three times and even daily to priests and religious. The latter term includes women religious, for can. 490 states that the laws of the canons for religious, when speaking in the masculine gender, apply likewise to religious women, unless the contrary is clear from the context or from the nature of the law.

"*Infirmis decumbentibus,*" i. e. those who are confined to their beds on account of disease, weakness, old age or any infirmity. Not only to those just mentioned but to the following, is this privilege extended, viz., to those who on account of the nature of their malady, cannot lie down, v. g., in certain cases of heart trouble. Vermeersch, Capello and Noldin give a broad interpretation of *decumbentes* and would include those who, while suffering from some illness or disease, were nevertheless able to go to the church.[65] Of course the other conditions imposed by the faculty would have to be present.

It is to be noted that priests are permitted to receive Holy Communion daily, not to say Mass.[66]

"*Non servato ieiunio,*" etc. According to a declaration of the Holy Office, Sept. 7, 1897, "*per modum potus*" may be understood so as to permit one to take broth, coffee and other liquids to which might be added meal or ground toast, provided the mixture does not lose its liquid state.[67] A raw egg or one only slightly boiled

64. Cappello, *De Sacramentis* I, p. 373, n. 506; Vermeersch, *Epitome*, II, p. 71.

65. Vermeersch, *Epitome*, II, p. 70; Cappello, *De Sacramentis*, I, n. 506.

66. Vermeersch, *Periodica*, XI, p. (87); Cappello, *De Sacramentis*, I, p. 374; Noldin, *De Sacramentis*, III, p. 174.

67. *Collectanea S. C. P. F.* n. 1983.

are considered by such authors as Capello and Vermeersch as taken "*per modum potus.*"[68] Medicine, whether taken "*per modum potus*" or otherwise, is also permitted by the faculty.

The faculty makes no mention of a necessity for breaking the fast as a requsite for its use and therefore it cannot be denied those who might, though perhaps with some little inconvenience, observe the fast.

17. Conferendi, rationabili de causa, Ordines minores omnes simul, etiam cum prima tonsura.

If the vicar or prefect apostolic has episcopal consecration he is equal to diocesan bishop in matters of ordination. If he is without the episcopal character, he may nevertheless confer tonsure and minor orders upon his own subjects and upon others who have the dimissorial letters required by law, but only in his own territory and during his time of office. Ordinations conferred which exceed the limits of the law are null and void.[69] As stated in another chapter, Vermeersch and Augustine are both of the opinion that the dimissorial letters are a requisite for the validity of the ordination of those who are not their own subjects.[70]

Canon 978 §3 states that without permission from the Holy See it is not allowed to confer tonsure and a minor order or all the minor orders on the same day. The faculty, however, permits the Ordinary not only to confer all the minor orders on the same day, but even tonsure and the four minors.

There should be a reasonable cause, for example, the desire to avoid an interruption in the studies of the students, or for the greater convenience of the vicar or prefect.

---

68. Vermeersch, *Epitome*, II, p. 71; Cappello, *De Sacramentis*, I, p. 375, n. 507.

69. Canon 957.

70. Cfr. Chapter III, p. 15.

18. Conferendi iusta de causa, omnes *sacros Ordines,* etiam presbyteratum, diebus ferialibus etsi continuis.

According to can. 1006, major orders should be given during Mass on the Ember Saturdays, the Saturday before Passion Sunday or on Holy Saturday, but for grave reasons the bishop may confer the major orders on a Sunday or holy day of obligation.

Between the last minor order and sub-deaconship there should be a year's interval or interstice, between sub-deaconship and deaconship, deaconship and priesthood, three months, unless the necessity or utility of the Church, according to the prudent judgment of the bishop, demands otherwise.[71]

According to the faculty, the major orders, including the priesthood may be given on any day, even a ferial. It moreover dispenses with the interstices so that all the major orders could be conferred on three successive days, i. e. sub-deaconship one day, deaconship the next, and priesthood on the third, even if all three days were ferials.

"*Iusta de causa,*" for example, the inconveniences entailed by sending the *ordinandi* to the bishop on three different occasions, or the difficulties of travel which the bishop would otherwise be compelled to undergo.

Since this faculty is given to prefects as well as to vicars apostolic, and the former are generally without the episcopal character, they therefore cannot *per se* confer the major orders but could have their subjects ordained by a bishop and at the same time making full use of the faculty.

19. Dispensandi gravi tamen de causa, cum utriusque cleri *diaconis* super *defectu aetatis* decem et octo mensium, ut, eo non obstante, ad S. Presbyteratus ordinem promoveri possint, dummodo idonei sint, et dimidiam partem quarti anni cursus theologici rite, secundum Codicis praescriptiones can. 976, absolverint.

71. Canon 978 §2.

Sub-deaconship is not to be conferred before the completed twenty-first year of age, deaconship before the completed twenty-second, priesthood before the completed twenty-fourth.[72]

The faculty allows the Ordinary to dispense deacons from the age required by law for the priesthood to the extent of eighteen months, i. e. deacon shall have reached the age of twenty-two years and six months completed. The faculty in no wise dispenses from the age required for either sub-deaconship or deaconship.

"*Utriusque cleri,*" and therefore not only members of the secular clergy but also religious, even the exempt.

The faculty demands that the prescriptions of the Code in can. 976 be fulfilled, viz., that the priesthood shall not be given until the second semester of the fourth year of theology. The same canon requires that the theological course should not be made privately but in class and according to the plan of studies laid down in can. 1365. The other qualities becoming the priestly state are demanded of the subject.

"*Gravi tamen de causa,*" i. e. not merely the desire of the deacon to be ordained but rather a real need of priests in the territory.

The Ordinary, whether vicar or prefect apostolic, may use this faculty in behalf of those who belong to his territory or are being ordained for it.

*20. Dispensandi, canonicis existentibus causis, super *impedimentis matrimonialibus* sive minoris sive maioris gradus (c. 1042), tam publicis quam occultis, etiam multiplicibus, iuris tamen ecclesiastici: exceptis impedimentis provenientibus ex sacro Presbyteratus ordine, ex defectu praescriptae aetatis et ex affinitate in linea recta, consummato matrimonio.

"*Concedendo tamen has dispensationes, Ordinarius prae oculis habeat regulas statutas in Codice, a can.* 1035 *ad can.* 1080, *circa impedimenta*

72. Canon 975.

in genere et in specie et, in impedimentis mixtae religionis et disparitatis cultus, servatis conditionibus ab Ecclesia praescriptis: videlicet de amovendo a catholico coniuge perversionis periculo, ac de universa prole utriusque sexus in catholicae religionis sanctitate baptizanda et educanda; monita parte catholica de obligatione, qua tenetur, conversionem coniugis acatholici prudenter curandi; eaque lege ut, neque antea neque post matrimonium coram Ecclesia initum, partes adeant ministrum falsi cultus ad matrimonialem consensum praestandum vel renovandum. Si agatur vero de matrimoniis cum hebraeis vel mahumetanis, peculiari ratione oportet ut constet de status libertate partis infidelis, ad removendum periculum polygamiae; absit periculum circumcisionis prolis; et si civilis actus sit ineundus, sit tantum caerimonia civilis nullaque Mahumetis invocatio aut aliud superstitionis genus interveniat."

This faculty may be sub-delegated and hence it is necessary that not only the Ordinary but the missionaries also should have a clear and thorough understanding of its import.

Before discussing the faculty, it would be well for the sake of completeness and a better comprehension of the powers given by the faculty, to call attention to canons 1043-1047 of the Code. Therein the Ordinary, the pastor or quasi-pastor, the priest who assists at the marriage, and the confessor, are given extraordinary powers to dispense from matrimonial impediments in the following circumstances:

1) In the urgent danger of death;

2) When an impediment is discovered after all the preparations have been made for the nuptials and the marriage cannot, without the probable danger of grave evil, be deferred until a dispensation can be obtained from the Holy See;

3) For the validation of a marriage already contracted, should there be the same danger in delay with no time for recourse to the Holy See.

Besides making the two exceptions found in can. 1043, the faculty adds a third, viz., the want of the required age. The faculty allows one to dispense from all the impediments of ecclesiastical law, regardless of whether they are diriment or prohibitive, major or minor, public or occult, and even though they are multiple. The three exceptions already alluded to, are: defect of the age required, viz., 16 completed years in males, 14 in females; the impediment arising from the order of holy priesthood; and affinity in the direct line if the marriage from which the affinity arose was consummated. This latter impediment has frequently been a little confused in the minds of some and therefore an illustration will help to give a clearer understanding of it. A man who married a widow who had a daughter from a former marriage, after the wife's death now wishes to contract marriage with her daughter. The impediment of affinity in the direct line is present and the question is, whether or not his marriage with the deceased woman was consummated.[73] If the answer is in the affirmative, it is a case of the impediment of affinity in the direct line "*consummato matrimonio*" and the Ordinary cannot, by virtue of his faculty, dispense in the case. If, on the contrary, the marriage is proven not to have been consummated, the Ordinary can use the faculty to dispense from the impediment of affinity in the direct line "*matrimonio non consummato,*" and thus the man would be free to marry the daughter (from a former marriage) of his deceased wife.

---

73. If the parties have lived together after the marriage has been contracted, its consummation is presumed in law until the contrary is proved. can. 1015 §2.

The matrimonial impediments of ecclesiastical law comprehended in the faculty are: simple vows;[74] legal relationship;[75] mixed religion;[76] disparity of worship;[77] Holy Orders;[78] solemn vows;[79] abduction;[80] crime;[81] consanguinity in the second and third degrees of the collateral line;[82] affinity in the collateral line;[83] public decency;[84] and spiritual relationship.[85]

Impediments which do not come under the faculty are those of the divine and the natural law, viz., impotency, *ligamen,* consanguinity in every degree of the direct line and in the first degree of the collateral line, i. e. between brother and sister.

Error, coercion, fear and ignorance are causes or circumstances which militate against the matrimonial consent and are not numbered among the matrimonial impediments of the Code.

The faculty mentions can. 1042, which discriminates between impediments of minor grade and those of major grade. Under the former class are: collateral affinity in the second degree; collateral consanguinity in the third degree; public honesty in the second degree; spiritual relationship; and the impediment of crime arising from adultery with a promise to marry, or with an attempt to contract even a civil marriage. All the other impediments are of the major grade.

It is necessary to bear the distinction in mind for the reason that a dispensation from a minor impediment is always valid inasmuch as it is not vitiated either

74. Canon 1058.
75. Canon 1059.
76. Canons 1060-1064.
77. Canons 1070 and 1071.
78. Canon 1072.
79. Canon 1073.
80, Canon 1074.
81. Canon 1075.
82. Canon 1076 §2.
83. Canon 1077.
84. Canon 1078.
85. Canon 1079.

because of the suppression of the truth (*subreptio*), or because of the assertion of falsehood (*obreptio*).

"*Canonicis existentibus causis.*" In the dispensation certain reasons or canonical causes must be alleged for the granting of the same. These are cited by the authors who treat the subject of Matrimony in Moral Theology or Canon Law, and have been taken from an Instruction of the Sacred Congregation of Propaganda, May 9, 1877.[86]

In the dispensations from the impediments of mixed religion and disparity of worship, more grave and serious reasons are required. The Congregation of Propaganda has admonished those delegated by the Holy See that only "*iustae gravesque causae*" should influence them to grant a dispensation for mixed marriages.[87] The same spirit is embodied in the new legislation in can. 1061 ff. and can. 1071. For a dispensation from the impediment of mixed religion, the following are recognized as justifying causes:

(1) The predominance of heretics or schismatics in the given region;

(2) a written promise made by the heretic to embrace the Catholic faith after marriage;

(3) the desire to avoid scandal, concubinage, defamation, or an attempt at marriage;

(4) the fact that such a marriage is the only means whereby the children of a former marriage can be educated in the Catholic faith.[88]

---

86. *Collectanea S. C. P. F.* n. 1470. For a more detailed discussion of these canonical reasons, cfr. Cappello, *De Sacramentis* III, p. 279, n. 259; Noldin, *De Sacramentis*, III, p. 702, n. 614.

87. *Litt. Encycl. S. C. P. F.* 11 March, 1868—*Collectanea, S. C. P. F.* n. 1324.

88. Zitelli, *De Disp. Matrimonialibus*, p. 60; Cappello, *De Sacramentis*, III, n. 314.

For a dispensation from the impediment of disparity of worship, the following may be alleged, viz., the predominance of infidels in the certain country and also Nos. 3 and 4 of those mentioned above. There are others which may be used but such reasons as superadult age, lack of dowry, poverty of the widow, "*angustia loci,*" enumerated in the Instruction of Propaganda already referred to, do not suffice singly, but when several concur in the same case the circumstances may justify the granting of a dispensation.

Besides the grave reasons required, the Church grants no dispensation from the impediments of mixed religion and disparity of worship unless the non-catholic party gives guarantees (*cautiones*) that the danger of perversion for the Catholic party will be removed, and both parties promise that all their children will be baptized and brought up as Catholics. There must be moral certainty that the guarantees will be observed and they should regularly be made in writing.[89] These *cautiones* or guarantees are necessary for the validity of a dispensation granted by virtue of this faculty from the impediments of mixed religion and disparity of worship.[90]

In view of the extraordinary conditions existing in China, the Holy Office, April 5, 1918, granted a special dispensation for that country as to the manner of exacting the *cautiones* required for a dispensation from the impediment of disparity of worship.[91] The unusual conditions are as follows:

(1) On account of the situation in that region, marriages between Catholics and infidels, especially between Catholic men and pagan women, are frequently unavoidable;

---

89. Canons 1061 and 1071.

90. Vermeersch, *Periodica*, XI, p. (121) (d); Blat, *De Rebus, pars* I, p. 725; Cfr. also, *S. C. S. Off.* 12-13 June, 1912—*A. A. S.* IV, 442; 21 June, 1912, *A. A. S.* IV, 442.

91. "*Sacerdos in Sinis,*" *a.* 1918, p. 232.

(2) It is sometimes impossible to exact the *cautiones* of the pagan woman; many times most difficult; frequently it is an occasion of harm;

(3) By reason of the customs of that region, only the *cautiones* given by the men are so binding as to make their fulfillment morally certain.

The Holy Office urged that the decree of June 12, 1912,[92] be observed as far as possible, but when the *cautiones* cannot be obtained in writing from a pagan woman, they are at least to be made orally. The Sacred Congregation then went on to say that in the event that this could not be done, it was left to the prudence and to the conscience of the Ordinaries to decide in each case whether or not the *cautiones* were equivalently contained in one of the following ways:

(1) The serious promise of the woman to embrace the Catholic faith;

(2) Her enrollment in the catechumenate;

(3) The laws or customs of the people which allow the wife no power over the religious education of the children, which depends upon the husband.

In all these cases, however, the *cautiones* are required of the Catholic party and the dispensation is not to be granted unless there is moral certainty of their fulfillment. The letter concludes by granting a "*sanatio*" for any marriages which perchance may have been invalid for lack of the "*cautiones.*"

It must be borne in mind that the indult given above is intended for China only and is not general legislation.

In marriages with Jews and Mohammedans the faculty requires;

(1) That the freedom of the infidel to marry be ascertained so as to avoid the danger of polygamy;

---

92. *A. A. S.* IV, 442.

(2) that there will be no danger that the offspring will have to undergo the rite of circumcision. The reference is to circumcision performed as a religious rite and not as a prophylactic measure;

(3) if a civil ceremony must be performed it must be strictly of a civil nature without any invocations to Allah and without the least semblance of superstition.

*21. *Sanandi in radice,* iuxta regulas in Codice a can. 1133 ad can. 1141 statutas, matrimonia ob aliquod impedimentum, de quo supra N. 20, nulliter contracta. Quod vero attinet ad prolis legitimationem, Ordinarius prae oculis habeat can. 1051.

The *sanatio in radice* of marriage is its validation carrying with it besides a dispensation from, or a cessation of an impediment, dispensation from the law requiring a renewal of the consent, a retroaction to the past with reference to the canonical effects.[93] A *sanatio* can be given only by the Apostolic See.[94]

The faculty allows a *sanatio* to be given for a marriage null and void by reason of the presence of any impediment mentioned in the foregoing faculty, viz., any impediment of ecclesiastical law, even though multiple, occult or public, major or minor, except three, namely, the one arising from the order of the holy priesthood, that arising from the lack of the required age, 16 completed years in males, 14 in females; and thirdly, the one arising from affinity in the direct line when the marriage has been consummated.

Any marriage entered into by both parties with a consent which naturally suffice but is juridically ineffective on account of an impediment of ecclesiastical law, or on account of the lack of the prescribed form may be validated by a *sanatio in radice,* provided the consent perseveres. The Church, however, does not grant a *sanatio* for a marriage contracted with an impediment

93. Canon 1138 §1.
94. Canon 1141.

of the divine or natural law and even after the impediment has ceased, not even from the moment of its cessation.[95]

The authors require a grave cause for recourse to a *sanatio*, as for instance when one or both parties are in ignorance of the impediment whose existence cannot be revealed without grave inconvenience, or if one of the parties cannot be induced to renew his consent so that the marriage can be validated in the usual manner or when a number of marriages are to be validated and the *sanatio* offers the more practical solution.[96]

The faculty calls attention to canons 1133-1141, but as canons 1133-1137 treat of simple validation and canons 1138-1141 of the *sanatio*, the former are most likely mentioned in order that one may see just how the *sanatio* is differentiated from the simple validation of invalid marriages and so to determine when the *sanatio* should be resorted to.

The offspring, with the exception of adulterine and sacrilegious, born or conceived by the parties in question are legitimated *ex tunc*, i. e. from the time the marriage was contracted although the marriage becomes valid only at the moment the *sanatio* is granted.[97]

***22. *Sanandi* pariter *in radice matrimonia mixta* attentata coram magistratu civili vel ministro acatholico.**

At first sight one may fail to see the necessity for this faculty and think that it is included in the preceding. But faculty No. 21 concerns only marriages which have been properly contracted with the prescribed form, but are null and void because of the presence of one or more impediments.

The faculty is dealing with a case of an attempt at a mixed marriage when the parties have appeared before

95. Canon 1139.
96. Noldin. *De Sacramentis, III*, p. 767, n. 666; Cappello, *De Sacramentis*, III, p. 904, n. 853.
97. Canons 1138 §1, and 1051 .

a non-catholic minister or a civil magistrate and the marriage is invalid because of the want of the prescribed form, commonly known as clandestinity.

If the marriage was attempted not before a civil magistrate but before a non-catholic minister contrary to the prescriptions of can. 1063 §1 and the excommunication *latae sententiae* reserved to the Ordinary was incurred, absolution from the censure would have to be obtained. This absolution should be given *in foro externo* unless the attempted marriage was secret and there is no danger of it becoming publicly known.[98]

If a dispensation had not been obtained from the impediment of mixed religion must the *cautiones* be exacted under penalty of refusing the *sanatio?* From a decision of the Holy Office, Dec. 22, 1916, it would appear that the power of *sanandi in radice* mixed marriages, null because of the lack of form, presupposes that the *cautiones* have been given, otherwise a new faculty must be obtained especially for such cases.[99]

*23. Dispensandi cum gentilibus et infidelibus *pluribus uxoribus* habentibus, ut post conversionem et baptismum, quam ex illis maluerint, si etiam ipsa fidelis fiat, retinere possint, nisi prima voluerit converti.

The next four faculties, all of which are sub-delegable, are concerned with what is known as the Pauline Privilege by virtue of which, a converted infidel whose wife remains in infidelity and refuses to cohabit with him, or will not do so *sine contumelia Creatoris,* i. e. without offering insult to the Creator, may contract another marriage and thus his first marriage, although consummated, becomes *ipso facto* dissolved. However,

98. Canon 2319 §1. However can. 66 §3, referring to habitual faculties such as the one we are discussing here says that faculties carry with them the right to use all the means necessary for their exercise. Hence the faculty of dispensing includes the power to absolve from censures, but only for the purpose of rendering the subject capable of receiving the dispensation.

99. *A. A. S.* IX, 13.

this privilege does not extend to the case of the marriage between a baptized and an unbaptized person contracted with a dispensation from the impediment of disparity of worship.[100]

The Pauline Privilege was promulgated by the Apostle St. Paul in favor of the faith.[101] The marriage contracted in infidelity is not dissolved by the fact of baptism but it is the second marriage contracted in Christianity that dissolves the one contracted in infidelity.[102]

According to can. 1125, matters pertaining to marriage in the constitutions, "*Altitudo*" of Paul III isued on June 1, 1537, "*Romani Pontifices*" of Pius V isued on August 2, 1571, and that of Gregory XIII, "*Populis,*" January 25, 1585,[103] although originally intended for particular countries, are to be extended to other regions where similar conditions prevail.

While the faculty makes mention of a polygamous husband, which is the more comomn, it is likewise applicable to a woman in a polyandrous union.[104] The faculty dispenses a converted polygamist from the necessity of making the second of the two interpellations prescribed in can. 1121. Only a negative answer to the first interpellation, namely an unwillingness on the part of his first wife to become a convert, is a sufficient reason for the baptized convert to enter into marriage with any of his consorts or pseudo-wives, provided the one he selects, embraces the true faith.

When the first wife is willing to be baptized, he must marry her. Should none of his wives be willing to embrace the Catholic faith, a difficulty arises. At first sight it would seem that the Ordinary need only give a

---

100. Canon 1120 §3.
101. I Cor. VII, 12-15.
102. Canon 1126.
103. These Constitutions can be found in the supplement to the Code under *Documenta* VI, VII, VIII.
104. *S. C. P. F.* 14 January, 1793—*Collectanea, S. C. P. F.* n. 611.

dispensation from the impediment of disparity of worship and let him marry another pagan woman. But this cannot be done without a special faculty for the reason that the faculty under consideration imposes the condition that the party selected, become a Catholic.[105]

*24. Dispensandi *super interpellatione* coniugum in infidelitate relictorum pro omnibus *casibus ordinariis,* dummodo scilicet adhibitis antea omnibus diligentiis, etiam per publicas ephemerides, ad reperiendum locum ubi coniux infidelis habitat, iisque in irritum cessis, constet saltem summarie et extraiudicialiter coniugem absentem moneri legitime non posse, aut monitum infra tempus in monitione praefixum suam voluntatem non significasse.

Prior to the Code the faculties for dispensing from the interpellations were known as ordinary and extraordinary;[106] the present faculty is an example of the former, the one which follows immediately, of the latter.

The faculty contains a dispensation from the two interpellations but it is restricted to ordinary cases and certain conditions are required for the validity of the dispensation.

In the first place every prudent effort must be made even through the medium of the press, to find out where the infidel party is in residence. If all the endeavors are fruitless then it must be ascertained at least by a summary and extra-judicial process that the absent consort could not be legitimately warned or that she failed to intimate her will within the time specified.

In practice therefore the interpellations may be dispensed with as often as the whereabouts of the infidel party remain unknown after a careful investigation has been made or when the said party resides in distant regions and safe access is barred, or when he or she fails to express his mind within the prescribed time, or finally,

---

105. *S. C. S. Off.* 22 November, 1871—*Collectanea* n. 1377, *ad Quaesitum secundum.*

106. Cfr. *S. C. S. Off.* 29 Nov., 1882—*Collectanea S. C. P. F.* n. 1581.

when it is morally certain that it would be useless to make the interpellations.[107]

The interpellations should regularly be made at least in the summary extra-judicial form by the authority of the converted party's Ordinary, who should grant time for consideration at the request of the infidel consort, with a warning, however, that failure to answer within the specified time will be taken as a reply in the negative.[108]

The infidel party should be summoned by letter to the ecclesiastical court where in the presence of the judge he or she may give an oral answer to the two questions or interpellations. The letter should not lack the customary formalities characteristic of official documents. The name of the summoned, of the summoner, and of the judge should be contained therein together with concise information as to the nature of the case. The time and place at which the summons was served and at which the person cited must appear, are all to be clearly stated.[109]

In connection with dispensations from the interpellations it is to be noted that they have the effect of upholding the validity of the marriage even if subsequent investigation should disclose the fact that the infidel party was prevented from declaring his or her mind, or even if he or she had embraced the true faith at the very time the second marriage was contracted.[110]

*25. Itemque dispensandi super *interpellatione* coniugis in infidelitate relicti, siquidem certo constiterit, saltem summarie et extraiudicialiter, interpellationem fieri non posse sine evidenti *gravis damni* aut coniugi iam ad fidem converso, aut christianis inferendi periculo.

This faculty is known as extraordinary and formerly was only given for a certain number of cases.[111]

107. Vermeersch, *Periodica*, XI, p. (139).
108. Canon 1122 §1.
109. Petrovits, The New Church Law on Matrimony, p. 405.
110. *S. C. S. Off.* 4 Feb. 1891—*Collectanea S. C. P. F.* n. 1746.

Although the consort is within reach and the interpellations can be made, they are nevertheless dispensed with when there is moral certainty that they will be the occasion of serious annoyance and persecution to the converted party or to the Christians.

It need scarcely be mentioned that it is the danger of harm which must be certain, not the harm itself. A presumption only would not suffice. Moreover, it is not necessary that the danger threaten the lives of the converted party or the Christians; it need only affect their liberty or their fortune, and not necessarily all of the Christians, but one or two at least.[112]

In this case likewise, the summary and extrajudicial process must be made to ascertain by positive proofs the existence of the danger of harm to the prospective convert, or to the Christians.[113]

*26. Permittendi ut, accedente gravi causa *interpellatio* coniugis infidelis *ante baptismum* partis quae ad fidem convertitur fieri possit; nec non, gravi pariter de causa, ab eadem interpellatione, ante baptismum partis quae convertitur, dispensandi, dummodo hoc in casu ex processu saltem summario et extraiudicialiter constet interpellationem fieri non posse, vel fore inutilem.

According to can. 1121, the interpellations are to be made after the baptism of the party who embraces the faith, although their validity would not be endangered should they be made before the reception of baptism.

The faculty is twofold. For a grave reason it permits the interpellations to be made before the baptism of the party who intends to enter the Church. Likewise for a grave reason and when it can be ascertained by a summary and extrajudicial process that the interpellations cannot be made, or that it would be useless to make them, the faculty dispenses with them entirely.

---

111. Cfr. *S. C. S. Off.* 29 Nov., 1882—*Collectanea S. C. P. F.* n. 1581.

112. Iglesias, *Brevis Commentarius*, p. 87.

113. *S. C. S. Off.* 29 Nov. 1882—*Collectanea S. C. P. F.* n. 1581, ¶ "*Verum sive*" etc.

B. Absolutions, Blessings, Indulgences, etc.

*27. Absolvendi ab omnibus *censuris,* sive simpliciter sive speciali modo Romano Pontifici reservatis.

Canon 2237 allows the Ordinary to absolve either *per se* or *per alium* from the censures reserved *simpliciter* to the Holy See, but only in occult cases. The faculty gives very ample powers of absolution and is intended for both the internal and external forum. It may be subdelegated to the missionaries.

"*Ab omnibus censuris,*" whether excommunications, suspensions or interdicts, and from which the Ordinary and the priests delegated by him may absolve without the necessity of obtaining the *mandata.* The censures reserved *specialissimo modo* are not included in the faculty.

While no special conditions are exacted by the faculty, there are those of the Code regarding the removal of scandal, the reparation due, and the formula of absolution.[114] These, however, are not necessary for the valid use of the faculty.

In connection with this faculty there was no occasion to mention those censures reserved to the Ordinary since he has the power of communicating the power to absolve from them.

*28. Dispensandi vel commutandi *vota privata* Sedi Apostolicae reservata, de quibus in can. 1309.

For any good reason the Ordinary of the place, may dispense his own subjects and *peregrini* or strangers, from private vows which are not reserved, provided the dispensation does not injure the acquired rights of a third party.[115] This power can be delegated by the Ordinary to his priests.

---

114. Cfr. Canons 2248 §2 and 2250 §3.
115. Canon 1313.

By virtue of the faculty which can be sub-delegated, the power is given to dispense or commute into a lesser work, the two private vows mentioned in can. 1309, which are reserved by law to the Holy See. These are the vow of perfect and perpetual chastity, and the vow to enter a religious Order with solemn vows. The law stipulates that these vows must have been taken unconditionally and after the completion of the eighteenth year of age.

Canon 1320 is deserving of mention here, inasmuch as it gives to those who have the power to annul, dispense or commute vows, the same power regarding promissory oaths, except in the case when the dispensation from the oath entails a prejudice to others who are unwilling to remit the obligation, in which circumstances only the Holy See can dispense for reasons of necessity or utility to the Church.

***29. Benedicendi solo crucis signo, sum omnibus Indulgentiis a S. Sede concedi solitis, *coronas* precatorias, *cruces,* parvas *statuas* et sacra *numismata,* et adnectendi coronis Indulgentias, quae a S. Birgitta et quae a Patribus Crucigeris nuncupantur.**

The indulgences referred to above as granted by the Holy See are known as Apostolic indulgences and have been accruing for centuries. At the beginning of his pontificate each Pope usually has a list published in which slight changes are frequently made and further indulgences granted. That of the present Pope may be found in the "*Acta Apostolicae Sedis,*" XIV, 143.

Certain conditions are mentioned therein which are worthy of mention. In order to gain the indulgences it is sufficient if one carry the indulgenced article about on his person or keep it in his home. Beads, rosaries, crosses, crucifixes, statues, medals, etc., must not be made of the following substances: tin, lead, glass or paper. The statues must be the representations of canonized saints or those commemorated in the martyrology.

The priest has only to make one sign of the cross over the articles to be blessed with the intention of attaching to them all the indulgences. It is not even necessary to pronounce the words aloud.[116]

30. Conferendi uni alterive ex suis sacerdotibus facultatem *consecrandi* iuxta formam in Pontificali Romano praescriptam *calices, patenas et altarium lapides,* adhibitis tamen oleis ab Episcopo catholico benedictis.

No one can validly perform consecrations who is not a bishop unless the faculty is given him either by law or by indult of the Holy See.[117] Vicars and prefects, even those without the episcopal character, may consecrate chalices, patens and portable altars with oil blessed by a bishop, but only in their own territory and during their tenure of office.[118]

The faculty allows the Ordinary to sub-delegate this power to a few of his priests and thus lessen his burdens. Whereas the "*uni alterive*" is understood by some to mean more than just one or two, i. e. to a few stationed at various points, the number depending upon the size of the mission and the need,[119] Blat is inclined to a stricter interpretation and would limit the number to two at the most.[120]

The Roman Pontifical has made no provision for such a faculty and supposes that the consecrations are to be made by a bishop. Wherefore the priest making use of the faculty will not follow the Pontifical too literally regarding the use of the mitre, etc.[121] Let him wear the surplice and white stole. The form remains unchanged just as given.

---

116. Iglesias, *Brevis Commentarius,* p. 96.
117. Canon 1147.
118. Canon 294 §2.
119. Vermeersch, *Periodica,* XI, p. (124); Iglesias, *Brevis Commentarius,* p. 98.
120. Blat, *De Rebus,* III, p. 728.
121. *Pontificale Romanum, tit. De patenae et calicis consecratione.*

Canon 294 §2 regarding vicars and prefects apostolic, cited above, mentions that the oil must be blessed by a bishop; the faculty says Catholic bishop and therefore Vermeersch would allow oils blessed by a bishop of another rite to be used if a bishop of the Latin rite could not be had.[122]

Canon 1148 §2 may be described as pertinent as it states that consecrations and blessings, both invocative and constitutive, are invalid unless the form prescribed by the Church is used. Under the latter class of consecrations come those for chalices, patens and altar stones.

While mentioning altar stones, it might not be amiss to remind the Ordinary that can. 1200 allows him to delegate a priest to consecrate altars, even those which are immovable, when they have lost their consecration. The short form is to be used and it may be very conveniently found in the "*Acta Apostolicae Sedis,*" XII, 449.

*31. *Erigendi* pium exercitium *Viae Crucis* ritu ab Ecclesia praescripto, cum applicatione omnium Indulgentiarum, quae huiusmodi exercitium peragentibus a Summis Pontificibus impertitae sunt; et applicandi easdem Indulgentias crucibus et crucifixis, pro infirmis aliisque legitime impeditis, prae oculis habito Decreto S. Poenitentiariae diei 14 decembris anno 1917.

Both residential and titular bishops from the time that they receive authentic notification of their promotion to the episcopate, are privileged to erect the Stations of the Cross in churches and oratories, even those which are private and also in other pious places which are used for devotional purposes. On behalf of those who are prevented from making the Way of the Cross, they may bless and apply to crucifixes all those indulgences granted by the Holy See for making the Stations.[123] However, they cannot sub-delegate this faculty to their priests, for it seems quite clear from

122. *Periodica,* XI, p. (124).
123. Canon 349 §1, n. 1 & 239 §1, n. 6.

a response of the Apostolic Penitentiary that the privileges accorded bishops in canon 349 §1 n. 1, cannot be sub-delegated.[124]

In this *Formula Tertia Minor* destined for those without the episcopal character, the faculty is given and is sub-delegable; in the *Formula Tertia Maior* it is found in the Supplement, and therefore what the vicars apostolic as bishops, have by law in canon 349, may be sub-delegated.

The faculty is twofold; in the first place it gives the power to erect the Stations, and secondly, the power to bless crosses and crucifixes and attach to them the indulgences for making the Way of the Cross. By its very nature the faculty for erecting the Stations is limited to the territory of the one possessing it, whereas the crosses and crucifixes may be blessed and indulgenced in the territory for all the faithful there and also for *peregrini*. Outside the territory in question it could be used only in behalf of the subjects of the Ordinary.

Ordinarily the Stations should be erected within a church, a public or semi-public oratory, in pious places such as convents, seminaries, etc. They may, however, be erected in the open, v. g. in a cemetery or cloister.

The faculty to erect the Stations must be given in writing unless it is contained in the faculties given the priest by the vicar or prefect. The written permission of the latter must be obtained each time the Stations are to be erected, together with the consent of the pastor of the church, the superior of the hospital, convent, etc., for the permission of the Ordinary and the respective pastor or superior must be had in writing before the Stations are blessing, otherwise the blessing is null and void. If the pastor himself is going to bless the Stations, he needs only the permission of the Ordinary, but

124. *Resp.* 18 July, 1919, *A. A. S.* XI, 332.

assistant priests must always have the pastor's consent or authorization.[125]

To gain the indulgences, three conditions are necessary: a brief meditation on the Passion in general; the Stations must be visited successively and without a notable interruption, and there must be a passing from one Station to the other. No particular prayers are prescribed. When many are making the Way of the Cross in common, only one person need make the round of the Stations while the others remain in their places and make the responses. A long pause or interruption is permitted in order to hear Mass or to go to Confession or Communion, without losing the indulgences.[126]

The second part of the faculty states that the indulgences for making the Way of the Cross may be attached to crosses and crucifixes. The priest need only make the simple sign of the cross over them with the intention of imparting all the indulgences. The use of these indulgenced crosses and crucifixes is restricted to those who are prevented by infirmity or otherwise lawfully hindered from making the Stations in a church. The conditions are that, whilst holding the cross or crucifix in their hands they meditate briefly on the Passion and say a *Pater* and *Ave* for each Station, concluding with the *Pater, Ave* and *Gloria* said five times in honor of the Five Wounds, and one *Pater, Ave* and *Gloria* for the Holy Father. Those who are too ill to recite the prayers just mentioned, need only make an act of contrition adding the invocation: "*Te ergo quaesumus tuis famulis subveni, quos pretioso sanguine redemisti,*" and to follow mentally the recitation, by another, of the *Pater, Ave* and *Gloria*, repeated thrice.[127]

---

125. Sleutjes, *Via Crucis, nn.* 32-34.

126. *S. C. Indulg.* 16 Dec. 1760—*Collectanea S. C. P. F.* n. 437 n. 4; Sleutjes nn. 52-54.

127. Sleutjes, *Via Crucis*, nn. 62-67. cfr. *Decr. S. Paenit. Apost.* 14 Dec., 1917, *A. A. S.*, X, 30.

32. Impertiendi, praeter concessionem de qua in can. 914, ter in anno in solemnioribus festis *Benedictionem Papalem* iuxta praescriptam formulam cum Indulgentia plenaria ab iis lucranda, qui vere poenitentes, confessi et S. Communione refecti eidem Benedictioni interfuerint, Deumque pro S. Fidei propagatione et iuxta mentem Summi Pontificis oraverint.

Canon 914 allows vicars and prefects apostolic to bestow the papal blessing with a plenary indulgence attached, once a year on one of the more solemn feasts. By virtue of the faculty, they may bestow the blessing thrice yearly.

On the part of the faithful it is required that they be present for the blessing and also that they have been to Confession and Communion and finally that prayers be offered to God for the spread of the faith and for the intention of the Sovereign Pontiff. Unless otherwise specified, the prayers to be said for the intention of the Holy Father are left to the choice of the individual.[128]

Prelates who have the use of the *pontificalia* should use the formula given in the *Caeremoniale Episcoporum*. For the others the formula is that of the *Rituale Romanum, tit.* VIII, *cap.* 32.

33. Concedendi ut, servatis consuetis conditionibus, *Indulgentiam Plenariam* in *primae Communionis* sollemni distributione et in S. Confirmationis administratione, christifideles ad S. Communionem vel Confirmationem rite accedentes lucrari possint.

A plenary indulgence may be granted to the faithful on the day of their first solemn Holy Communion and on the day they receive Confirmation.

"*Solemni,*" i. e. when the ceremony is attended with special solemnity. Thus children, adults also, who had made their first Communion on the sick bed or privately, could on this occasion receive Holy Communion and so gain the indulgence.

---

128. *S. C. Indulg.* 23 May, 1841, ad. 3—*Collectanea S. C. P. F.* n. 922; cfr. *S. C. Indulg.* 13 Sept. 1888, ad. 2—*Collectanea S. C. P. F.* n. 1693.

"Rite accedentes," i. e. free from excommunication and in the state of grace, etc.

The usual conditions are demanded as explained in a previous faculty.

*34. Concedendi *"Indulgentiam Plenariam* primo conversis ab haeresi, servatis consuetis conditionibus.

The missioners to whom this faculty has been sub-delegated, may grant a plenary indulgence to converts from heresy.

"Primo conversi ab haeresi," viz., those who were baptized and reared in a heretical sect and who have now abjured their heresy in the external forum. It does not apply to converts who have lapsed into heresy again and afterwards returned to the faith.[129] Nor is the indulgence applicable to converts from paganism or infidelity, or to invalidly baptized Protestants converts, as baptism remits everything and there is no need of the indulgence.[130]

A person baptized and reared in the Catholic Church who obstinately denies or calls into doubt any of the truths of the Catholic faith is a heretic,[131] and Blat is of the opinion that he, too, could gain the indulgence upon his rejection of the heresy and reconciliation with the Church.[132]

The conditions required are the usual ones, Confession, Communion, etc.

35. Impertiendi *Indulgentiam Plenariam singulis* singulis ex clero, qui per quinque saltem dies *Sacris Exercitiis* interfuerint, ac, sacrosanctum Missae sacrificium celebrantes, vel saltem ad S. Synaxim accedentes, pias ad Deum preces effuderint pro S. Fidei propagatione et iuxta mentem Summi Pontificis.

The conditions mentioned are:

---

129. Konings—Putzer, *Commentarium*, p. 253.
130. Konings—Putzer, p. 253; Blat, *De Rebus* Pars. 1, p. 294.
131. Canon 1325 §2.
132. Blat, *De Rebus* III, p. 293.

(1) That the retreat last five days. Since the faculty does not insist on five whole days, it will suffice if the retreat open the evening of the first day and close the morning of the fifth;[133]

(2) the clerics must be present at the exercises, which should be conducted in common. Clerics is to be understood in the broad sense, i. e. even those with first tonsure. It would include members of both the religious and secular clergy;

(3) to gain the indulgences the reception of Holy Communion or the celebration of Mass is required together with the prayers for the spread of the faith and for the intention of the Sovereign Pontiff.

*36. Concedendi Benedictionem Apostolicam cum *Indulgentia Plenaria* omnibus christifidelibus, qui spiritualibus Exercitiis seu *Sacris Missionibus,* de quibus in can. 1349, §1, ultra medietatem interfuerint, benedictioni cum Cruce in fine postremae concionis impertiendae vere paenitentes, confessi ac sacra Communione refecti adstiterint, atque ecclesiam, in qua conciones huiusmodi habebuntur devote visitaverint, ibique per aliquod temporis spatium pias ad Deum preces effuderint pro sanctae Fidei propagatione et iuxta mentem Summi Pontificis.

It is the duty of the Ordinaries to see that the pastors and quasi-pastors have a mission given to their parishioners at least every ten years.[134]

The faculty permits the papal blessing with a plenary indulgence to be given on this occasion.

No time is set for the length of the mission and in some places they last a week, or if two weeks, then one week for the men, the other for the women.

To gain the indulgence, the faithful must have attended more than half the exercises of the mission and they must be present for the blessing after the last sermon. Moreover it is required that they have been

133. Vermeersch, *Periodica* XI, p. (99).
134. Canon 1349 §1.

to confession and Communion, and on the occasion of a visit to the Church where the mission is being held, pray for the spread of the faith and for the intentions of the Holy Father. One Our Father and one Hail Mary devoutly said would fulfill the latter requirements.[135]

*37. Concedendi in actu *visitationis* paroeciarum, quasi-paroeciarum et missionum, nec non communitatum tam saecularium quam religiosorum, ut *Indulgentiam Plenariam* una vice tantum lucrari possint christifideles dummodo contriti, confessi ac S. Communione refecti pias ad Deum preces fuderint pro. S. Fidei propagatione et iuxta mentem Summi Pontificis.

Vicars and prefects apostolic are to visit their districts whenever necessary, and if unable to go in person they may send another in their place.[136]

The faculty gives the Ordinary the power of imparting a plenary indulgence on the occasion of his canonical visitation. It is sub-delegable and hence the indulgence may be imparted by the priests, v. g. the pro-vicar or the pro-prefect or the deans, who act as substitutes.

The indulgence can be given only once during each visitation of the parishes, quasi-parishes, mission stations, hospitals, orphanages, convents, even of exempt religious, etc. From can. 927 it would seem that *peregrini* or strangers could also gain this indulgence.

The conditions are the usual ones imposed and have already been explained.

*38. Concedendi christifidelibus ut *Indulgentias,* propter quas *Confessio* saltem bis in mense requiritur, lucrari possint, etsi ob legitimum impedimentum inde a mense ad poenitentiae sacramentum non accesserint.

The faithful who are in the habit of confessing at least twice a month unless legitimately impeded, or who receive Holy Communion daily in the state of grace

135. *S. C. Indulg.* 13 Sept. 1888 ad 2;—*Collectanea S. C. P. F.* n. 1693.

136. Canon 301 §2.

and with a good and holy intention, even though they miss once or twice a week, may gain all the indulgences without actual confession for which otherwise confession would be a necessary condition. The indulgences of an ordinary or extraordinary jubilee are exceptions to this rule.[137]

The faculty modifies the requirements of can. 931 §3 just cited, to the extent that the faithful by a monthly confession,[138] may gain the indulgences for which otherwise bi-monthly confession is required. The jubilee indulgences would likewise be exceptions to the faculty.

"Ob legitimum impedimentum," for instance, the absence of the priests, or on account of the great distance to their habitation. Vermeersch brings out a good point when he says that even if for a period of three or four days there was ample opportunity to go to confession, a person would not be obliged to confess twice within the same week in order to comply with the prescriptions of can. 931 §3.[139]

The power given in this faculty is not restricted to individual cases, but may be extended by general indult to the faithful at large.

*39. Concedendi ut omnes praedictae *Indulgentiae* applicari possint *per modum suffragii* animabus in purgatorio detentis.

According to can. 911, indulgences are granted both for the living and for the dead, but in the latter case they are applied in the form of suffrage (*per modum suffragii*). Those inferior to the Roman Pontiff cannot grant indulgences applicable to the poor souls unless by indult of the Holy See.[140]

By virtue of this faculty all the indulgences granted in the faculties from numbers 32-38 may be applied to the poor souls in purgatory.

---

137. Canon 931 §3.
138. The time is reckoned according to can. 34 §3, nn. 1, 3.
139. *Periodica*, XI, p. (102).
140. Canon 913 §2.

The conditions are the same as stated in each faculty the only difference being in the intention of the one who gains the indulgence.

***40. Benedicendi crucifixos cum Indulgentia plenaria vulgo *toties quoties* nuncupata: idest a quocumque ex fidelibus in mortis periculo constitutis lucranda. Grassantibus autem epidemicis vel contagiosis morbis, concedendi ut fideles *in periculo .mortis* constituti *Indulgentiam Plenariam* lucrari possint, Christi crucifixi imaginem vel crucem deosculando; vel, ea deficiente, Ssmum Iesu nomen corde saltem, si ore non potuerint, invocando.**

This faculty which is sub-delegable may be used in behalf of the subjects of the Ordinary, whether clerical, lay or religious, wherever they may be and in behalf of all those actually residing in his territory.

The "*toties quoties*" indulgence attached to crucifixes, was explained by the Holy Office to mean that any of the faithful "*in articulo mortis*" could gain a plenary indulgence by kissing or holding in his hand one of the indulgenced crucifixes, even if it were not his own. It was required that he had been to confession and Holy Communion. If no such crucifix was available, the indulgence might nevertheless be gained by devoutly invoking the Holy Name of Jesus, if not orally, at least in one's heart.[141]

The faculty is really twofold. In the first place it gives the power of attaching the "*toties quoties*" indulgence to crucifixes with the simple sign of the cross, so that under the conditions required by the Holy Office just described, any of the faithful may gain the indulgence. There is this difference, however. Whereas the declaration of the Holy Office demands that the party be "*in articulo mortis,*" the faculty reads "*in periculo mortis.*"

"*Grassantibus autem epidemicis,*" etc. The faculty now provides for extraordinary circumstances. Thus,

141. *Declaratio S. C. S. Off.* 11 June, 1914, *A. A. S.* VI, 347.

when epidemics, plagues, etc., are raging, on account of the great numbers who fall victims, the faculty allows the plenary indulgence to the faithful in danger of death from the disease or from other causes, who kiss any crucifix, cross, image or picture of Christ crucified, or if these are not to be had, by simply invoking the Most Holy Name of Jesus, if not aloud, "*corde saltem.*"

It is to be noted that in both cases the persons need only be in the danger of death, i. e. when they are sick or infirm and there is a probable danger of death.

41. Concedendi ut, expleto Divino Officio diei, legitima concurrente causa, privatim recitari possit *Matutinum cum Laudibus* diei sequentis, *statim post meridiem.*

This faculty is not delegable and therefore the permission must be given by the Ordinary himself.

"*Expleto Divino Officio diei.*" Although Vermeersch is of the opinion that the ablative absolute does not express a condition *ad validitatem,* nevertheless in this instance he maintains that unless one has finished the office of the day he cannot use the faculty of anticipating at midday. He bases his opinion upon inquiries made at the Congregation of Propaganda.[142] Other commentators, Blat, for example, hold that it is only *ad liceitatem,*[143] while Iglesias sees an opportunity for *epikeia.*[144]

"*Legitima concurrente causa.*" Any of the reasons advanced by the authors as justifying the anticipation of vespers and compline before midday would suffice in this case also, v. g. on account of studies, greater convenience, pressure of duties, etc. In fact, Vermeersch and Putzer both hold the opinion of Marc that one using a privilege of this kind without any reason whatever,

142. *Periodica,* XI, p. (75).
143. *De Rebus,* III, p. 774.
144. *Brevis Commentarius,* p. 122.

would satisfy his obligation but would be guilty of a venial sin.[145]

The faculty is restricted to the private recitation of the Office and therefore is applicable to all those who are not bound by law to the public recitation in choir. Those who do not fall under this latter class, yet out of devotion are in the habit of reciting the Office in common after the manner of those in choir, may likewise use the faculty for such recitation still remains private.

In determining noon or midday, one may follow the local time, true or mean, or the legal time, regional or extraordinary.[146]

42. Concedendi ut ob legitimam gravemque rationem, de qua eius conscientia oneratur, *loco Divini Officii, Rosarium* vel aliae preces recitari possint.

The moralists give several reasons which excuse one from the obligation of the Divine Office, such as physical impossibility, serious illness, etc.,[147] but the faculty does not dispense from the obligation but merely substitutes for a legitimate and grave reason, a lesser work, viz., the Rosary or its equivalent in prayers.

"*Ob legitimam gravemque rationem.*" Such reasons as poor sight, severe headaches, etc., would always be sufficient, but there are others such as long hours in the confessional or in catechising and in this regard the Ordinary is free to determine under what circumstances the Rosary may be substituted for the Office. Inasmuch as the recitation of the Breviary is a grave obligation there must be a grave reason to substitute for it, in whole or in part, a lesser work.

Does the faculty mean five or fifteen decades of the Rosary? In answer to this question, the Holy Office,

145. *Periodica,* XI, p. (104); Konings-Putzer, *Commentarium,* p. 307, n. 173.

146. Canon 33 §1.

147. Cfr. St. Alph. *Lib.* VI, *cap.* II, n. 154; Noldin, III, p. 803, n. 705.

July 2, 1884,[148] replied that the complete Rosary of fifteen decades was to be understood. However, it was left to the judgment of the bishop to decide under what circumstances and with what persons, the five decades or its equivalent in prayers could be substituted.

As to the prayers which may be said instead of the Office, the Sacred Penitentiary declared that those whose eyesight was failing and who could read only with great difficulty or those who suffered severe headaches from the slightest reading should substitute for the parts of the Office, the following prayers: in place of *Matins,* the beads and at least the psalm *Miserere* and the *Benedictus;* for each of the Hours, seven Our Fathers and seven Hail Marys with the *De profundis;* for Vespers, twelve Our Fathers and twelve Hail Marys, with the psalm *Dixit Dmnus* and the *Magnificat;* for Compline, seven Our Fathers and seven Hail Marys with the psalm *Qui habitat* the canticle *Nunc dimittis*, and the *Credo.*[149]

The above is only given by way of suggestion in the event that the Ordinary may have reasons for commuting from part of the Office only.

43. Permittendi suis missionariis ut *vestes laicales* induere possint, si aliter vel transire ad loca eorum curae commissa, vel in eis commode permanere non potuerint.

All clerics are obliged to wear a becoming clerical dress in accordance with the legitimate customs of the place and the rules of the Ordinary.[150]

Religious should wear the habit of the Order or Congregation both in the house and when on the outside, unless a weighty reason excuses them, according to the judgment of the higher, or, in urgent cases, of the local superior.[151]

---

148. S. C. S. Off. 2 July, 1884 *ad* 8—*Collectanea S. C. P. F.* n. 1622.
149. Konings-Putzer, *Commentarium*, p. 290, n. 168.
150. Canon 136 §1; cfr. can. 2379.
151. Canon 596.

By virtue of this faculty the Ordinary may permit his priests, including religious, to adopt the customary lay dress in their travels about the mission, or during their residence there, when it would be otherwise inconvenient.

44. Permittendi suis missionaries ut *artes medicinae et chirurgiae* exercere valeant, dummodo in illis periti sint, operentur absque incisione, praeterquam ad sanguinem emittendum, et nihil exigant pro huiusmodi exercitio; et in curandis mulieribus ea vitent, quae sanctitatem characteris, quo insigniti sunt, dedecent.

Clerics may not practice medicine or surgery without an apostolic indult.[152]

Under the following conditions which are all essential, the Ordinary may permit his priests to practice medicine or surgery:

(1) Provided that they are skilled, i. e. not to the extent of professional doctors and surgeons, but with sufficient skill and knowledge so as not to put the patient's life in danger;

(2) No incisions may be made except for blood-letting.

(3) The work must be done gratuitously. This would not prevent their accepting a nominal sum to cover the expenses of dispensary upkeep;

(4) Whatever medical or surgical attention is given to women, must be entirely compatible with decency and befitting the clerical state. The Ordinary may take the occasion to lay down any precautions which he may deem expedient.

The reason for the second prohibition probably lies in the fact that the Holy See wishes the priests to avoid

152. Canon 139 §2.

the danger of incurring the irregularity mentioned in can. 985 §6.

45. *Assignandi pensionem* quasi-parochis vel missionariis ex infirmitate resignantibus quasi-paroecias vel missiones, in quas per decem annos incubuerunt, solvendam annuatim a successore, non excedentem tertiam partem fructuum quomodolibet provenientium ex quasi-paroeciis vel missionibus, deductis expensis.

The Ordinary cannot burden parochial benefices with pensions unless they are in favor of the pastor or parochial vicar of that very parish who has retired from office. The pension, however, must not exceed one-third of the revenues after expenditures have been deducted.[153]

By virtue of this faculty, the Ordinary may assign a life time pension to a priest who has resigned from his quasi-parish or mission on account of his infirmities. The priest must have put in ten years of service in the parish and his retirement is necessitated only by infirmity or illness; no other cause is admitted by the faculty.

The pension is to be paid annually by his successor and should not exceed one-third of the revenues, including the stole fees, after the expenses of worship and general upkeep of the Church have been deducted.

*46. Dispensandi cum catholicis pauperibus, qui opera sua valde indigent, ut *serviliter laborare* valeant *diebus Dominicis,* exceptis Paschate et Pentecoste, post tamen S. Missae auditionem si possit audiri, si vero non possit, recitatis precibus suppletivis.

Ordinaries and pastors, *a pari* quasi-pastors or missioners, in individual cases and for good reasons can dispense individual subjects or individual families, even outside of their territory and *peregrini* or strangers within their territory from the obligation of keeping the holy days of obligation.[154]

---

153. Canon 1429 §2.
154. Canon 1245 §1.

The faculty which is sub-delegable is an extension of the Ordinary's power but it is concerned only with the servile work forbidden on Sundays. In behalf of the faithful who are poor, the faculty allows them to be dispensed, even habitually, from the obligation of abstaining from servile work. This dispensation may be promulgated by a public proclamation if the Ordinary so desires.

The conditions imposed are as follows: (1) That the faithful are poor and are in great need of the income derived from their extra labor allowed by the faculty; (2) the dispensation is given for Sundays only, Easter and Pentecost excepted; but the faculty does not hold for the other holy days of obligation; (3) work is permitted only after they have heard Mass, unless this is impossible, when they should substitute the recitation of prayers which in most cases the Ordinary prescribes, v. g. the recitation of the Rosary or some of the litanies.

C. For the Ordinary Himself

47. Fruendi *indulto* personali *altaris privilegiati* quotidiani, dummodo intuitu huius privilegii, nihil omnino, praeter consuetam eleemosynam percipiat.

Although the term Ordinary would include the vicar delegate, these faculties are personal in the sense that they are given to the person of the Ordinary, i. e. prefect apostolic, rather than to the office. Therefore they are not enjoyed by the vicar delegate.

All bishops, even titulars, have this privilege by law.[155] Here it is given to Ordinaries without the episcopal character. The privilege consists in this, that in whatever place or on whatever altar they celebrate, their Mass is privileged and a plenary indulgence applicable only to the poor souls, is obtained *per modum suffragii* for that soul for whom the Mass is offered.

---

155. Canon 349 §1, n. 1 & can. 239 §1, n. 10.

Canon 918 §2 states that a larger stipend cannot be asked for Masses said on a privileged altar and the faculty make this a condition for its valid use.

48. *Lucrandi Indulgentias,* quas aliis vi facultatum sibi concessarum impertiendas censuerit, impletis tamen conditionibus.

49. *Utendi* ipse *personaliter,* in iisdem tamen adiunctis, *facultatibus* seu permissionibus, quas, intra limites in praecedentibus articulis expressos, concedendas esse censuerit.

ANIMADVERSIONES

I. Praedictae facultates ea lege conceduntur, ut non omnes indiscriminatim *subdelegari* possint, sed illae tantum quae asterisco* notantur, seu quae habentur sub numeris: 14, 16, 20, 21, 22, 23, 24, 25, 26, 27, 28, 29, 31, 34, 36, 37, 38, 39, 40, 46.

II. Ordinarius insuper supradictis omnibus facultatibus sive per se sive per alios uti tantum valet *intra fines suae iurisdictionis;* easque gratis et sine ulla mercede exerceat, et facta mentione apostolicae delegationis.

III. Quod si forte *ex oblivione vel inadvertentia* ultra tempus supra praefinitum, seu ultra . . . hisce *facultatibus* Ordinarium *uti contingat,* absolutiones, dispensationes, concessiones omnes exinde impertitae uti ratae atque validae habeantur. Insuper *datis* ab Ordinario *precibus pro renovatione* seu prorogatione facultatum, ipsae in suo robore *perseverare* censeantur, usquedum responsum S. C. ad eumdem Ordinarium pervenerit.

The observations have been explained in the Preamble to the faculties. They are the same for the three Formulae except the members in I, which correspond to those faculties which may be sub-delegated.

SUPPLEMENTUM PRO FORMULIS MINORIBUS

The Sacred Congregation of Propaganda is accustomed to add some supplementary faculties. For the *Formulae Minores* they are as follows:

1. Erigendi *illas etiam* Confraternitates *a. A. Sede approbatas quarum instituendarum ius Apostolico ex privilegio*

aliis reservatum est (c. 686 §2), *una excepta Confraternitate* SSmi *Rosarii, iisque ascribendi christifideles;* ac benedicendi coronas et scapularia earundem Confraternitatum *propria, cum applicatione omnium Indulgentiarum et privilegiorum quae Summi Pontifices iisdem Confraternitatibus impertiti sunt.*

The faculty allows the erection of the Confraternities whose erection is reserved to the Holy See by can. 686 §2, the one exception being that of the Confraternity of the Most Holy Rosary. The Third Orders are not included in this faculty because they are not confraternities.[156]

Ordinarily the mere erection does not suffice in order that the members of the confraternity may gain all the indulgences, but it is further required that it be aggregated to an arch-confraternity. Here it is evident that aggregation is unnecessary and its erection alone is sufficient.

The Ordinary receives the power to bless the beads and scapulars proper to each confraternity and of attaching to these objects the special indulgences.

As it is given here, the faculty may not be subdelegated and hence a decree of the Ordinary is necessary for the erection of any of the confraternities.

2. Subdelegandi *suis missionariis facultatem ascribendi confraternitatibus de quibus supra* n. 1, *christifideles; ac* benedicendi coronas et scapularia earundem Confraternitatum propria, *cum applicatione omnium Indulgentiarum et privilegiorum quae Summi Pontifices iisdem Confraternitatibus* impertiti sunt.

The preceding faculty to erect Confraternities approved by the Holy See, etc., cannot be sub-delegated. But this faculty, no. 2, allows the missionaries to inscribe (only) members in the aforementioned Confraternities and to bless and attach the indulgences to the beads and scapulars.

---

156. Cfr. Canons 700 & 701 §1.

3. Benedicendi, *ritibus tamen ab Ecclesia* praescriptis, omnia (cetera) scapularia a Sede Apostolica probata, eaque imponendi sine onere inscriptionis.

Hanc pariter facultatem Ordinarius suis missionariis subdelegare potest.

Since the Ordinaries to whom *Formula Tertia Minor* is granted are not bishops, they have not this faculty by law. By virtue of this faculty the Ordinary and his priests may bless all scapulars approved by the Holy See and invest the faithful without, however, the obligation of enrollment which is ordinarily required, in order that the faithful may gain the indulgences.

The scapulars referred to here are all those which are not proper to any confraternity and therefore would not come under the preceding faculty, v. g. the Scapulars of the Sacred Heart, St. Joseph, the Hearts of Jesus and Mary.

II. Formula Tertia Maior

This formula which is given to Ordinaries with the episcopal character, does not differ substantially from the *Formula Minor.* However, faculty no. 2 of the *Formula Tertia Maior* is the one given below. Other differences will be noted as they occur.

2. Conficiendi *olea sacra*[157] cum sacerdotibus, quos potuerit habere; et, si necessitas urgeat, etiam extra diem Coenae Domini.

The holy oils required in the administration of the various Sacraments must have been blessed by the bishop on the preceding Holy Thursday, nor are the old oils to be used except in the case of necessity.[158]

When the supply of the holy oils is about exhausted, other olive oil which has not been blessed may be added

157. *i. e. oleum catechumenorum, oleum infirmorum et sacrum chrisma.*

158. Canon 734 §1.

but always in lesser quantity than the holy oils themselves.[159]

The faculty dispenses with respect to the time and in the number of priests and ministers required by liturgical law for the blessing of the oils, viz., twelve priests, seven deacons and seven sub-deacons. Instead the bishop may avail himself of those priests who are at hand, and if there is urgent necessity he may also consecrate the oils at other times during the year.

Faculty no. 31 of the *Formula Minor, "Erigendi pium exercitium,"* etc., is found in the supplement to the *Formula Maior.*

C. For the Ordinary himself

47. *Asservandi* in sacello domus stabilis suae residentiae *Ssmum Eucharistiae Sacramentum,* ea lege, ut lampas indesinenter ante tabernaculum lucescat, clavis diligenter custodiatur, aliaque iuxta liturgicas leges plene serventur.

Although the term Ordinary would include the vicar general or the vicar delegate, these faculties are personal, i. e. given to the person of the Ordinary, or vicar apostolic rather than to the office. Therefore they are not enjoyed by the vicar delegate.

The Blessed Sacrament may be reserved in his fixed residence and in the event that he passed several months of the year in different parts of his vicariate, the bishop could make use of the faculty in each case as soon as he took up his fixed abode.

The conditions under which this faculty is granted are those required by law, viz., in cans. 1265 §3, 1269, 1270, 1271 and 1272, which treat on the subject of reservation of the Blessed Sacrament.

Nos. 48 and 49 are the same as in the *Formula Minor.*

---

159. Canon 734 §2.

50. Utendi *throno* cum *baldachino* et *cappa magna* in Pontificalibus; nec non permittendi presbyteris in ecclesiis suae iurisdictionis celebrantibus ut sui *nominis* tamquam Antistitis sive in precibus ferialibus sive *in canone Missae* mentio fiat: quatenus haec ipsi a iure concessa non fuerint.

Only residential bishops have the right to erect the throne with the canopy in the churches of their diocese.[160] The faculty extends this privilege to vicars apostolic who are titular bishops and also allows them to wear the *cappa magna* in pontifical functions, i. e. in those ceremonies which according to the liturgical laws require the use of the crosier and mitre.[161]

Moreover they may permit all priests saying Mass in their churches to insert their name in the Canon after the words *Antistite nostro*, and also to insert their name in the ferial *preces*.

The privileges granted in this faculty were not given vicars apostolic by common law.

Supplementum pro Formulis Maioribus

Numbers 1 and 2 are the same as those found in the supplement *pro Formulis Minoribus.*

3. Subdelegandi *pariter suis missionariis sequentem duplicem* facultatem *quae eidem Ordinario, qua Episcopo,* in canone 349 §1, n. 1. *Conceditur, nempe*:

a) benedicendi, *ritibus tamen ab Ecclesia praescriptis,* omnia scapularia *a Sede Apostolica probata, eaque imponendi sine onere inscriptionis;*

b) erigendi, *ritibus pariter ab Ecclesia praescriptis, Stationes Viae Crucis, cum omnibus Indulgentiis quae huiusmodi pium exercitium peragentibus a Summis Pontificibus Impertitae sunt; et* applicandi easdem indulgentias crucibus et crucifixis *pro infirmis aliisque legitime impeditis,* prae oculis habito decreto S. Poenitentiariae 14 decembris anno 1917.

---

160. Canon 349 §2, n. 3.
161. Canon 337 §2.

The privileges given in can. 349 are granted to bishops from the time they receive authentic notification of their promotion to the episcopate.

The faculty under the letter a) is treated in no. 3 of the supplement *pro Formulis Minoribus;* that under the letter b) will be found under faculty no. 31 of the *Formula Tertia Minor.*

BIBLIOGRAPHY

Sources

Acta Apostolicae Sedis, Romae, 1909-1924.
Acta Sanctae Sedis, Romae, 1865-1908.
Canones et Decreta Concilii Tridentini, Romae, 1904.
Canonical Legislation Concerning Religious, Authorized English Translation, Rome, 1918.
Caeremoniale Episcoporum, Mechliniae, 1867.
Codex Iuris Canonici, Romae, 1917.
Codicis Iuris Canonici Fontes, Romae, 1923.
Collectanea Constitutionum, Decretorum, Indultorum, ac Instructionum Sanctae Sedis (Coll. Paris), Parisiis, 1880.
Collectanea Sacrae Congregationis de Propaganda Fide. 2 vol. Romae, 1907.
Decreta Authentica Congregationis Sacrorum Rituum, 6 vol. Romae, 1912.
Iuris Pontificii de Propaganda Fide vol. Romae, 1888.
Pontificale Romanum, 2 vol. Mechliniae, 1873.
Rituale Romanum, Taurini, 1917.

Authors

Alphonsus, St. Theologia Moralis, Ratisbonae, 1846.
American Ecclesiastical Review, Philadelphia.
Andreucci, Hierarchia Ecclesiastica, Romae, 1746.
Arregui, Summarium Theologiae Moralis, edit. 3a. Oniae, 1919.
Augustine, A Commentary on the New Code of Canon Law, 8 vol. St. Louis, 1922.
Baart, The Roman Court, 4th ed. New York, 1899.

Benedict XIV, De Synodo Diocesana, Prati, 1844.

Blat, Commentarium Textus Iuris Canonici, Lib. II, De Personis, Romae, 1921.

Blat, De Rebus III, Romae, 1924.

Bouix, De Curia Romana, Parisiis, 1880.

Brunnemanus Johannus, Commentarium in Codicem Justinianeum, Coloniae Allobrogum, 1771.

Cappello, De Sacramentis, 3 vol. Aug. Taurin. 1921-1923.

Catholic Encyclopedia, 15 vol. New York, 1907-1912.

Catholic Encyclopedia, Canon Law Supplement, New York, 1918.

Chelodi, De Personis, Tridenti, 1922.

Cocchi, Commentarium in Codicem Iuris Canonici, Lib. II, De Personis Taurinorum Augustae, 1922.

D'Annibale, Summa Theologiae Moralis, 3 vol. Romae, 1908.

De Herdt, Sacrae Liturgiae Praxis, 3 vol. edit. 7a, Lovanii, 1883.

Denziger, Enchiridion Symbolorum et Definitionum, Friburgi in Br. 1908.

De Smet, De Sponsalibus et Matrimonio, edit. 3a, 2 vol. Bruges, 1920.

Encyclopedia Britannica, Art. *Vicars*, vol. XXVIII, New York, 1910.

Ferraris, Bibliotheca Canonica, 9 vol. Romae, 1885-1892.

Gasparri, Pietro Card. Tractatus Canonicus de Matrimonio, 2 vol. Parisiis, 1904.

Gothofriedus, Jacobus, Commentarium in Codicem Theodosianum, Lapsiae, 1736.

Iglesias, Brevis Commentarius in Facultates S. C. P. F. Romae, 1924.

Konings-Putzer, Commentarium in Facultates Apostolicas, edit. 4a, New York, 1893.

Maroto, Institutiones Iuris Canonici, 2 vol. Romae, 1919.

Martin, The Roman Curia, New York, 1913.

Nainfa, The Costume of Prelates, Baltimore, 1915.

Noldin, Theologia Moralis, 3 vol. edit. 13a Oeniponte, 1921.
Ojetti, Synopsis Rerum Moralium et Iuris Pontificii, 4 vol. Romae, 1910.
Petrovits, The New Church Law on Matrimony, Philadelphia, 1921.
Pruemmer, Manuale Iuris Canonici, Friburgi, 1922.
"Sacerdos in Sinis," Pekini, 1918.
Sleutjes, Instructio de Stationibus S. Viae Crucis, edit. 4a, Ad Claras Aquas, 1909.
Vermeersch, De Formulis Facultatum S. C. de Propaganda Fide, Commentaria, Bruges, 1923.
Vermeersch, Epitome Iuris Canonici, 3 vol. Bruges, 1922.
Vermeersch, Periodica de Re Canonica et Morali, 1911-1923, Bruges.
Wernz, Ius Decretalium, Prati, 1915.
Wernz-Vidal, De Personis, Romae, 1923.
Ybanez, Directorium Missionariorum, Barcinonae in Hispania, 1921.
Zitelli, Apparatus Iuris Ecclesiastici, Ratisbonae, 1903.
Zitelli, De Dispensationibus Matrimonialibus, Romae, 1887.

UNIVERSITAS CATHOLICA AMERICAE

WASHINGTON, D. C.

FACULTAS IURIS CANONICI

1923-1924

No. 24

THESES

DEUS LUX MEA

THESES

QUAS

AD DOCTORATUS GRADUM

IN

IURE CANONICO

Apud Universitatem Catholicam Americae

CONSEQUENDUM

PUBLICE PROPUGNABIT

FRANCISCUS JOSEPH WINSLOW

SACERDOS SOCIETATIS AMERICANAE
PRO MISSIONIBUS EXTERIS

IURIS CANONICI LICENTIATUS

HORA XI A. M., DIE XXVIII MAII A. D. MCMXXIV

I.	Cans.	8-11	De Natura et Obiecto Legis Ecclesiasticae.
II.	Cans.	12-14	De Subiecto Legis Ecclesiasticae.
III.	Cans.	15-16	De Obligatione Legis Ecclesiasticae.
IV.	Cans.	25-30	De Consuetudine.
V.	Cans.	31-35	De Temporis Supputatione.
VI.	Cans.	38-47	De Vi Rescriptorum.
VII.	Cans.	51-59	De Rescriptorum Exsecutione.
VIII.	Cans.	63-65	De Privilegiorum Acquisitione.
IX.	Cans.	80-86	De Dispensationibus.
X.	Cans.	87-89	De Personis.
XI.	Cans.	90-95	De Domicilio et Quasi-Domicilio.
XII.	Cans.	96-98	De Consanguinitate et Affinitate.
XIII.	Cans.	111-117	De Excardinatione et Incardinatione.
XIV.	Can.	198	De Ordinario.
XV.	Cans.	201-202	De Iurisdictione.
XVI.	Cans.	295-298	De Iuribus Vicarii ac Praefecti Apostolici.
XVII.	Cans.	299-306	De Obligationibus Vicarii ac Praefecti Apostolici.
XVIII.	Cans.	309-311	De Coadjutoribus et Successoribus Vicarii ac Praefecti Apostolici.
XIX.	Cans.	750-754	De Subiecto Baptisimi.
XX.	Cans.	762-769	De Patrinis in Baptisimo.
XXI.	Cans.	1035-1042	De Impedimentis Matrimonii in Genere.
XXII.	Cans.	1043-1046	De Ordinariorum et Sacerdotum Potestate Dis-

			pensandi Urgente Mortis Periculo.
XXIII.	Cans.	1060-1064	De Impedimento Mixtae Religionis.
XXIV.	Can.	1068	De Impedimento Impotentiae.
XXV.	Cans.	1070-1071	De Impedimento Disparitatis Cultus.
XXVI.	Cans.	1081-1085	De Consensu Matrimoniali.
XXVII.	Cans.	1133-1137	De Convalidatione Simplici.
XXVIII.	Cans.	1138-1141	De Sanatione in Radice.
XXIX.	Cans.	1552-1555	De Iudiciorum Ecclesiasticorum Notione, Obiecto, et Divisione Ratione Obiecti.
XXX.	Cans.	1554-1933	De Causis Mixti Fori.
XXXI.	Can.	1560	De Foro Competenti Necessario.
XXXII.	Cans.	1561-1568	De Foris Voluntariis.
XXXIII.	Cans.	1572-1579	De Iudice Primae Instantiae.
XXXIV.	Cans.	1594-1596	De Tribunali Secundae Instantiae.
XXXV.	Cans.	1598-1601	De Competentia Sacrae Romanae Rotae.
XXXVI.	Cans.	1602-1605	De Competentia Signaturae Apostolicae.
XXXVII.	Cans.	1636-1639	De Loco et Tempore Iudicii.
XXXVIII.	Cans.	1742-1746	De Interrogationibus Partibus Faciendis.
XXXIX.	Cans.	2252-2253	De Absolutione a Censura extra Periculum Mortis.
XL.	Can.	2254	De Absolutione Censurarum in Urgenti Casu.

XLI. De Forma Regiminis Ecclesiae.
XLII. De Iure Romani Pontificis Exigendi Relationes Ordinariorum.
XLIII. De Iure Gladii.
XLIV. De Iure Ecclesiae Condendi Scholas.
XLV. De Iure Ecclesiae Praedicandi Fidem.
XLVI. De Iure Romani Pontificis Eximendi Personas et Territoria.
XLVII. De Iure Ecclesiae Possidendi Bona Temporalia.
XLVIII. De Potestate Romani Pontificis in Territorio Missionum.
XLIX. De Organizatione Regiminis Missionum.
L. De Iure Civili Quoad Matrimonium.
LI. The Nature of International Law.
LII. The Monroe Doctrine Not a Principle of International Law.
LIII. The Right of Intervention.
LIV. The Method of Acquisition of Territorial Jurisdiction.
LV. The Three Mile Limit or the Jurisdiction of a State Upon the Open Sea.
LVI. The Right of Fishing on the High Sea Belongs to all States Alike.
LVII. The Jurisdiction of the State over Vessels.
LVIII. Sovereigns Sojourning in Their Official Capacity in Foreign Countries are Exempt from Local Jurisdiction.
LIX. The Immunity from Local Jurisdiction Conceded Diplomatic Agents.
LX. Extradition in International Law.

* * * * * *

Vidit Facultas:

PHILIPPUS BERNARDINI, S. T. D., J. U. D., p. t. Decanus.

HUBERTUS L. MOTRY, S. T. D., J. C. D., p. t. a Secretis.

Vidit Rector Universitatis:

†THOMAS J. SHAHAN, S. T. D., J. U. L., LL. D.

BIOGRAPHICAL NOTICE.

Francis Joseph Winslow was born June 14, 1898, in Cambridge, Mass. After the completion of the secondary school training at Framingham, Mass., he entered, on Sept. 5, 1916, the Maryknoll Preparatory College at Clark's Green, Pa., and a year later the Major Seminary of the Catholic Foreign Mission Society of America. In the fall of 1922 he matriculated at the Catholic University of America, Washington, D. C., where, since his ordination on June 17, 1923, he has continued his studies under the direction of Rt. Rev. Filippo Bernardini, S. T. D., J. U. D.; Rev. Valentine T. Schaaf, O. F. M., J. C. D.; Rev. Hubert L. Motry, S. T. D., J. C. D., and Mr. Manoel de Oliveira Lima, L. H. B. To the Faculty of Canon Law he is happy, at this occasion, to express his sincere gratitude for their constant inspiration and guidance in the study of Church Law and, in particular, that part of it which has been made the object of special investigation in his dissertation.

www.ingramcontent.com/pod-product-compliance
Lightning Source LLC
LaVergne TN
LVHW050217080826
844660LV00012B/426

* 9 7 8 0 8 1 3 2 2 6 1 8 7 *